S0-BUA-849

Living with
the Spirits of the Land

Barbara Thomas

A SPIRITUAL MEMOIR
&
COUNCIL OF GNOMES PROJECT

Other Writings by Barbara Thomas

The Burned Woman
Celebrating the Magic of Jim's Road
Healing Burned Woman (DVD)
Council of Gnomes (Blog)

Acknowledgements

~ with heartfelt gratitude ~

Mary Jane Di Piero, editor
Gretchen McPherson, cover design
Andrea Boone, author photo and others, photo editing
Melody Culver, copyeditor

I DEDICATE THIS BOOK

To my intimate family

Who created a solid, loving base

Of conscious and unconscious support

As I answered the inner call

My parents, Zepha and Rex

My dear husband, Jim

Our wonderful children,

Peter, Anne, Donna, John

I live in gratitude
For all the beautiful people
Who have walked my path with me
For short and long periods of time.

I live in gratitude
For all of the angelic and elemental spirits
For Rama and Mano
Who have guided my whole earth path.

I live in gratitude
For my own willingness to walk my path
One step at a time,
Following, trusting the current guiding presence

Even though I didn't know
I was on a spiritual path .db.

I am grateful
For the core beliefs I have held in my awakening years
That which I need to know will be revealed to me
That which I need to have will be brought to me.

I am grateful
For snippets of guidance that I have followed
To the best of my ability.

Following spirit without hesitation
To be honest and open and free - to let people see who I really am
Takes the rawest kind of courage.*

Doors will be opened, and doors be closed
To get me where I need to be,
To do what I need to do.
I am grateful.

*John Powell, *Why am I afraid to tell you who I really am?*

CONTENTS

FOREWORD

Belief in the Unseen as Therapy for the World

It is everywhere apparent that we as the human species must radically change the way we live in order to come into greater harmony with ourselves and the natural world. How do we do this when the odds seem so stacked? Where must we go to actualize change within ourselves in the face of so much calling out for it? What guidance might we find when we seek answers to the challenging questions of our time? The greatest potential for illumination might arise from the most unlikely place, a small, offshoot scientific discipline called cryptozoology. Conventional definitions call it "the study of extinct, endangered or mythical creatures," or closer but still not quite right as "the study of beings as yet unproven by science." The definition, however, that really drives home the point of cryptozoology might be "the study of beings unseen by common means." It is the first discipline to take oral history of the unexplained into account as a form of truth.

It is in believing the unfathomable of another's experience that we serve as a bridge for that person's experience to become real, tangible, and grounded in a greater shared reality of what's possible. This is the gift of allowing cryptozoology to be what it could truly become—a scientific discipline that experiences unseen beings through oral account and catalogs the potentiality for the existence of these beings and their realms as truth. A willingness to believe is the key to it all.

They are and always have been here all around us as our intimate allies: the elves, faeries, gnomes, devas, elementals, and angels. They need us to believe in them, in ourselves, in order for them to participate in any of the guidance for which we have been asking. Theirs is a participatory art. Our eyes, our hearts, and our minds are the portals through which all of the unseen can converge and emerge from that participation. If you listen carefully enough, their voices are calling.

It is in this nature of belief as a bridge for the unseen to cross through us into our world that we may begin to access the empathy in our hearts and witness the stories in this Council of Gnomes Project by Barbara Thomas. It is through Barbara's willingness to work with these gnomes and share their knowledge that we are fortunate enough to have their help in remembering how to become the heaven-on-earth stewards we were always born to be.

Steven Odell
Rabbit's Moon Tea Arts

Steven Odell is a mutidisciplinary artist with a background in anthropology. This study has led him to a lifelong exploration into the relationship of societal beliefs and how they are informed by culturally relevant narratives of the times. Currently he is pursuing studies in the art of human relationships through the lens of Chinese tea culture in China and how this tea culture may build bridges between disparate communities. Steven currently resides in Portland, Oregon.

INTRODUCTION

MY NAME, BARBARA, MEANS "CHILD OF NATURE." This has been my soul call, to wake up and relate with the earth as Mother. My Mother Earth has introduced me to others of her children who live in the nonphysical world. I call this world Faerie, an ancient word used in Celtic cultures to describe the spirits of the earth–the many beings and levels of consciousness in nature. For close to 30 years I have lived within the heart of a redwood forest. On my land there is a sacred grove, known as the Amphitheater, where the veil between the worlds is very thin. The three realms of Faerie reign here, meet with humans here, become true and real here in this holy place. They have joined in circle dance with humans here for 22 years.

My life, my art, my writing, all reflect what I have learned from the angels and elementals who live on my land. There will always be people who know more, feel more, see more than I do. What I do know, what I have seen, what I have felt and experienced with these loving beings, I share with you. I am guided in this process by my Council of Gnomes. I officially met this Council in 2001 when, in my studio, I began to see—in my mind's eye–a gathering of beings requesting my participation. From then until now, each time I go to the studio to work I open Council first, to align with its spiritual presence and guidance. Throughout this practice, which included documenting the proceedings on my laptop, I soon had so much information that I wanted to create a little book. I have four starts in binders on my shelf. In 2010 I hired an editor to assist in the process, but soon I grew discouraged. Something was not right; I felt like I was getting off track. One thread of consciousness that has long guided me is, "When in doubt...DON'T." Heeding what I call a "sign along the highway", I put the book aside.

Mano, my principal gnome teacher, had higher priority projects in mind for me. The first was to create *Healing Burned Woman*, a DVD inspired by my book, *The Burned Woman*. The witch burnings during the Inquisition in Europe resulted in the elimination of many who lived consciously and harmoniously with nature. The lingering effects created by this purge manifested as individual fear from personal past-life experience, or as a fear simply held within the collective consciousness. This history, and the self-limitation and self-doubt it has embedded in the human psyche, have been important aspects in my life's work. The DVD has four parts: "Burned Woman's Story," which reproduces the book; "Barbara's Story," which relates my process of learning to be open to nature; "Nature's Story," which tells what Mother Nature has asked of me and how she wants to relate with people; and "Healing and Awareness Circle," which brings the other three parts into activity and practice. In this fourth part I was guided to create a workshop people can do on their own to create their own stories–a few people in a home, or a large group of people (which I have done many times).

Following the DVD project, Mano encouraged me to complete *Celebrating the Magic of Jim's Road*, a book of interviews that I had started earlier, in which people relate their experience of the amazing energy that radiates into the surrounding area from the vortex in the Amphitheater. These two projects taught me so much about my own process and offered an enormous healing I didn't even know I needed.

The Council of Gnomes blog, begun in April 2013, was the next project, instigated by Mano as another step in broadening human awareness of and engagement with the angelic and elemental worlds. This blog has been Mano's collaboration with me and Mary Jane Di Piero, who has presented the blog these past five years. (Council of Gnomes blog, www.barbarathomas.info)

Now, in 2018, I am back to writing the Council of Gnomes book, my spiritual memoir. Part of the excitement I am experiencing is seeing how my Council guides me to remember past experiences and writings that show me, over and over, how these preparatory adventures and insights add depth and clarity to my current project. Mano points out that these early experiences are an integral part of the story, clarifying how my Council has worked with me all of my life—certainly before the idea of a gnome or elemental held any reality for me.

In the first two parts, "Awakening to the Call" and "Meeting Mano: Learning to Trust", I look back from my perspective as a 90-year-old and see how ancient intentions, on my part and that of the elemental beings, made possible the third part of this book: "Working with the Council of Gnomes: Opening Portals of Awareness, 2001-2017." "Burned Woman's Story" and "The World of Faerie", parts four and five, are major themes in my spiritual memoir. Part 6, "Summer Journeys", recounts three summers of dedicated work in the Amphitheater and in my studio, and gives indications of future collaboration with the elemental realm. "Recurring Themes that Have Guided My Life", the final part, rounds out enduring topics that cross the timelines of my life, as well as giving samples of my spiritual pursuits.

Art has been a vital centering in my life, and in addition to the offerings that show themselves primarily through writing and speaking, the Council has also shepherded and inspired my studio and art projects. In 1973 in La Cañada I began creating a portal for my paintings of angels and gnomes. The Awakening Project, which lasted more than a year (2014 to 2016), resulted in five paintings of women whose eyes are open—a calling for women to wake up and stand in their power. My artistic practice has also, since 1977, included the transformational "squiggle drawings" and the ink-stick drawings initiated during my 2014-2016 summer journeys, which connected me ever more deeply with the spirits of the land.

The Journey Beckons

PART ONE

AWAKENING TO THE CALL

1927–1986

IN THE BEGINNING

MY COUNCIL OF GNOMES asked me to tell you this story of their engagement, over many years, with a willing and trusted human being, and what they had to do to help me remember my soul commitment to work with angels and elementals in service to Mother Earth. Here I share teachings the Council has brought me that show how they have guided me all of my life.

Angels, gnomes, and elementals were never a part of my childhood reality. My only contact was in fairy stories and the ugly garden statues of little men smoking pipes and pushing wheelbarrows. I did not like Rumpelstiltskin. "Snow White and the Seven Dwarfs" was my first experience of heartful connection with gnomes. I loved Dopey, appreciated Doc's wisdom, and identified with and felt sorry for Sleepy.

I grew up as an only child with three adults who were very different from one another. My mother was strong and practical and took the lead in the family. She had grown up on a small farm next door to her grandmother, who owned the land. Her goal was to become a businesswoman and have enough money to be comfortable. She also wanted to be a mother and decided that having one child would not interfere with her businesswoman plans. She saved money to buy a four-family flat in the heart of Los Angeles. Upstairs, our home was on one side and the office was set up on the other. The two downstairs apartments brought in enough money to pay the mortgage with a little extra. My father, more fun-loving and jovial than Mother, was also focused on being successful in business. He would have preferred a son rather than a daughter as his only child. Miss Quinn, the live-in housekeeper, was nunlike and silent. She sat in her room most of the day, coming into the family home for dinner and to do the dishes. Her job was to be present with me when business called Mom and Dad out at night to make house calls and sales. They were each focused on their own goal, and I learned to dance among their personalities.

Many years later, in an inner process of teaching me who I am and where I came from, Spirit would drop into my mind little rhymes or phrases that held enormous truth and revelation in a humorous, lighthearted way. Two such insights I remember just popping into my head while I was out in nature, walking on the land: "Deedle dum, deedle dee, Daddy wanted a boy, but what he got was me," and "You were an exuberant child raised in a household of repressed adults." I was intrigued and for the first time realized the truth of the situation. My only emotional response was, "Wow, that is really true!" I put the new revelations into a file of awareness—no trauma attached, just appreciation for insights that brought me knowledge of myself I had never thought of before.

They Watch & Guide Me

Early on, I remember having a feeling that I was part of a team living in Spirit—that I had been sent to earth as the team's human representative and the others would always watch over me and guide me along my path of service. I was working closely with my teachers Rama and Mano long before I actually met them; they were providing experiences that prepared me to recognize them when the time came.

They Guide Me Along My Path

An important young-adult experience of expanding my consciousness occurred in 1948 when I was 21. My neighbor Dorothy Rempel's father came to us with the news that post-war Europe was opening its doors to tourists. American Youth Hostel was creating tours for Americans to bicycle for two months with a European leader, staying in youth hostels each night. Dot and I were ready for the adventure of experiencing life beyond our Los Angeles home base and of observing firsthand the other-worldliness of war devastation.

We crossed the Atlantic on a student ship that was actually a troop transport with bunk beds three deep. Side by side, we

European Street Scene

were packed like sardines in a can. Of the many groups on the boat, one was the Marshall Plan in Action–youth going to clean up rubbish from bombed churches and public buildings and to help rebuild destroyed schools. The leaders offered classes on European History and French, which Dot and I attended–when we weren't simply hanging out with the other students.

Some hostels were bombed manor houses, some were buildings at the edge of a town, and others were in people's farmhouses with the owners acting as house parents. We met hostellers from other countries, spent our nights exploring the local areas, then rode off again in the morning. Our official tour went through Holland into Luxembourg, Belgium, France, Switzerland, and I don't know where else because our group staged a mutiny and separated from our leader. We were tired of the daily push to get from hostel to hostel and wanted freedom to follow our noses and truly explore. Dot and I hitchhiked, catching rides in big trucks that could take our bicycles. One time in France, on the way to Switzerland, we came out from eating in a restaurant and two men with a large truck said they could give us a ride. But they seemed to be fiddling around, and we noticed that the people in the restaurant were laughing. Suddenly I had a hit: Don't go with these men; they hate Americans and intend to drive off quickly, stealing our bikes.

We took a train to Paris for a week, then the train and ferry to London. There we sold our bikes to two Englishmen who toured us through London for another week. We were in Amsterdam for the big jubilee celebrating the canal lights being turned on for the first time after the war, and the change in monarchy from Queen Wilhelmina to her daughter Juliana. We joined some other students and went partying together all night until we ended up at the home of Hans, a local student, to sleep the little of the night that was left.

Dot and I each had a three-speed Raleigh bicycle, sleeping bag and saddlebags on the back with our clothes: one pair of slacks, one shirt, one long-sleeved shirt, bathing suit, pajamas, a skirt, saddle shoes, and bobby socks. I thought I was a strong, stable bike rider, but I found I really was quite wimpy and wanted to stop for lots of resting. When we were waiting for the border guard to go through all of the papers for our group to enter Luxembourg, I saw a little church and went inside to lie down on a bench to rest. I suddenly felt an amazing inflowing of love move through my whole body and said to myself, "OH! God is in this church." I thought about the war and how people must have prayed. Then I jumped up, realizing that my group would be leaving and no one knew where I was. This heavenly visitation in my twenties was fleeting, but later I marveled at the experience and at my casual, almost ho-hum acceptance of it. And I also knew absolutely that God had filled me with His love. It was a life-changing experience and the memory of it stayed with me.

Establishing Adult Life

Jim and I met at UCLA at a fraternity-sorority exchange. I was dancing and saw him standing along the wall, and I knew he would ask me to dance. Soon he tapped my partner on the shoulder and I stepped into his arms to continue the dance. We immediately became life partners and married in 1951. After I graduated, he still had two years of eligibility as a football player, and while he finished I worked for Beechnut Baby Food. I wore high heels, hat, and gloves, and always had a backache. My job focused on talking with mothers and doctors, which improved my skill of making conversation. I devised my own question-of-the-month for the doctors and in time observed that half of them would answer my question one way and the other half would answer it quite differently. This disagreement among the experts helped me learn to follow my own inclinations. After work I would sit in my car writing my work report and listening to a radio interview program. One of the interviews was with the author of the book *Answers Without Ceasing*, which was about having prayers answered. This was a new idea for me and it prompted me to begin reading books about healing and prayer. Jim received a scholarship for prospective real estate students and after graduation accepted a job in the appraisal department of Coldwell & Banker. We began raising our family.

I was gradually becoming more aware of a spiritual trajectory in my life and of the possibility that I had some task to discover. This time of awakening to my task occurred through and around my very active marriage, with growing children at home, and later with grandchildren, international travel, and service. It also included traveling and relating with Mother Earth in many parts of the world. I have been in all 50 states and have walked on the earth of 53 different countries. Even with his enormous skill, patience, and ingenuity in bringing books and people

into my life and in moving my family three times (always to the foot of a mountain), Mano still had to wait 20 years for me to "wake up" and move through my own personal fear that I was making it all up. I now see how my Council moved me from my Southern California homes of La Cresenta and La Cañada to the Central Coast ranch in San Luis Obispo, and then finally to my present home on the Mountain near Ben Lomond in Northern California.

The council managed to arouse my curiosity in the early 1960s when we were living in La Cresenta. By this time Jim and I had four children: Donna, Peter, Anne, and John. I found a small gnome statue, one inch tall, in a park where the children played. The next week I found another one at the beach, and later one on the school playground. I put one of them on my kitchen sink and talked with him when I did dishes. They were beginning to get my attention.

Also at this time I first heard my inner voice, which quite clearly said, "God is within you. Pat needs $20." At first I wondered where I would get the money. Then I remembered my piggy bank. I sat on the bed, using a knife in the slot, shaking the bank. The money rolled out. I had $19.50.

I was reading lots of books recommended by spiritual teachers, as I searched for models of humans living a God-centered life. It was the first time I had heard of reincarnation; my consciousness was beginning to expand.

LA CANADA YEARS

AFTER WE MOVED TO LA CAÑADA, bordered by the Angeles National Forest, the family became deeply immersed in the La Cañada Presbyterian Church. I was the Woman's Association president and started the first prayer group. As my field of spiritual interests expanded and I began to meet people in the community outside of the church, I had the inner knowing that I was to stay in that church as an anchor of stability for me and for my family. Later when the children were older we went to San Onofre to go surfing each weekend, so didn't attend church regularly during the summers.

Hazel Burrows' Meditation Group

I loved to participate in the Woman's Association study group discussions at the Presbyterian church. It gave me the opportunity to think things through and to speak out loud some of the thoughts stimulated by the books I had been reading. One day Alma Miller, a grand lady with a beautiful southern accent, regal manner, and a cane with a large gold handle, turned to me and said, "Barbara dear, to look at you no one would ever realize that you had such deep thoughts in your head." Quietly my heart laughed with joy and I said, "Thank you, Alma." I guess my daily miniskirts and large Sunday hat must have made an impression on her.

Margaret, also a member of the Woman's Association, was a quiet studious woman with a brilliant, inquisitive mind. She had also been aware of my inquisitive, open mind and one day said, "Barbara, I would like to invite you to my meditation group. Fred Kimble, an animal communicator, will be the guest. I think you would enjoy him and the people Hazel brings to her weekly group." She was correct; I loved it and continued going whenever possible. Our new church janitor, Gene Dorsey, also attended regularly. We became good friends and I often joined him for stimulating metaphysical discussions during the week as he cleaned the Sunday school rooms.

Studying with Gene Dorsey and Others

Gene had experienced a direct visitation with Jesus while flame-proofing the drapery around the painting of the Crucifixion at Forest Lawn Memorial Park in Glendale. From that point on, he went on a crusade to discover any evidence others had experienced with what he called "The Christ Event". In this search he collected a huge metaphysical library. Each time I visited him at church he would give me a stack of metaphysical books to read. I read more than 100 books in the first yearafter I met him. Donna, at the time the youngest of my three children, had just started kindergarten. I would begin reading as she walked out the door and put the book down when she returned home. I learned how to read without burning myself while I ironed clothes; I could knit and even do dishes while reading.

The books covered an amazing range of topics and authors, including Madame Blavatsky, Alice Bailey, Rudolf Steiner, and books about healing, direct voice mediumship, spacecraft, and extraterrestrial visitations. I found them stimulating and sometimes confusing. One day I complained, "Gene, I don't understand a word I am reading." In his composed and authoritative manner, he said, "That's okay, Barbara, just keep reading; your soul understands."

At that first meditation group meeting I saw Gene across the room talking with Fred Kimble. He later told me that when he had seen Fred looking deeply into my aura, he asked what he was observing. Fred told Gene that he'd never seen such a highly developed spiritual consciousness completely disconnected from the mental. As I write this book, I sincerely think that Gene's persistent encouragement of my reading arose from this observation. He wanted to educate my mind and hoped to facilitate a connection with my spiritual nature, which must have been developed in past lives but not until this point brought forward in this lifetime.

When Gene started working for the La Cañada Presbyterian Church, he asked if the church had any prayer groups. He was told, "No, but there is one woman interested in prayer, Barbara Thomas." The days I visited with Gene while he cleaned the Sunday school rooms, we prayed for the children and for the church. One of our conversations brought forth information that solved a mystery in my life and created another one. La

Cañada is located on the side of the Angeles Forest with many trees lining its curving streets and little lanes leading back into mountainous areas. One of these lanes pulled me like a magnet. I would go out of my way to pass it, driving slowly and looking down it as far as I could see.

I discovered that Gene had lived in the house at the end of the lane during his college years, with Anna and her daughter Florence. Anna was a medium; Florence and Gene were sweethearts. Each time they all sat for a session, a feminine spirit named Starlight would come through for a short connection, encouraging Gene and Florence to get married and have a baby. Starlight wanted to incarnate through the two of them. Gene was on the football team at USC and was not willing to give up his education or football to get married and start a family. Finally, one night a very sad Starlight

Starlight

spoke through Anna, saying she had to leave. She could wait no longer in her search for parents to bring her to earth. "Sometime I will find you," she said.

My curiosity about the little lane in the foothills of La Cañada was solved and a bigger question haunted me: "Am I Starlight? Is this really true?" I did not and never have told anyone this story. I prayed for clarity and got the thought to ask God if it were true. If I was the spirit named Starlight, I set the intention that the next time I went to Hazel's meditation group, someone would say the name "Starlight". Jim went with me to the next meeting. After the meditation he was telling the group that we would not be there next time because we were taking our first backpacking trip into the High Sierras. Hazel's husband told Jim about a flavorful brand of dehydrated food for backpacking, with the brand name of Starlight.

Sometime later Hazel invited Jim and me for dinner to meet Brenda Crenshaw, a well-known psychic, healer, and medium in the Los Angeles area. Brenda was very comfortable to be with, gracious and humorous with a solid, grounded, natural feeling about her. When dinner was over Hazel said, "All right, we are now going to hold hands to create a circle, so Brenda can go into trance and bring in some spirits." I didn't know this was going to happen and thought, *Oh my gosh, Gene Dorsey told me NEVER to hold hands for a séance.* What was I going to do? I had ingrained the practice of turning to God whenever I was in doubt. So I prayed, "Dear God, please protect me."

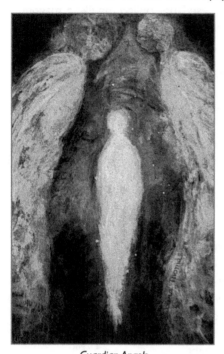

Guardian Angels

Brenda immediately said, "Barbara, I am seeing such an unusual sight. Two angels just entered the room and are wrapping you in blue gauze." This reinforced that when I ask for help, the angels come to answer my call.

Also during these La Cañada years, my friend Patricia Settles came each week to do healing work on me. She said that my light was blocked and worked to help connect my mental and spiritual selves. Through her inner vision she could see my large, golden light covered over with a black cloud. She described her work as pulling out the splinters–and pulling parts of myself back into the whole, even from past life experiences. She suggested that I could offer my life as a schoolroom in which spirit beings taught incarnating souls by watching my process.

Wednesdays with Brooks and Paul Lewis

Every Wednesday night for almost two years Jim and I were dedicated to dinner and meditation with Brooks and Paul. We alternated houses, and our children loved these nights. When the gathering was at our house they enjoyed the table conversations; on alternate weeks they loved being on their own. One night as we drove in I saw Anne run down the hall; inside, I discovered a warmed-up TV and Anne conveniently tucked into bed, pretending to be asleep. Watching television longer than I would normally let them was a secret pleasure.

Brooks and I had met years earlier at Hazel's meditation group and we often got together for tea, talk, and meditation. I found her fascinating. Her living-room wall was filled with small original paintings of the major arcana of the Tarot cards, and she had an elemental companion named oh den do.

A Curious Prophecy

Two packages arrived on the same day; each contained a book, and neither named the sender. One was mailed from California, the other from Colorado. I was mystified and fascinated when I realized the content of the two was similar. One, *A Clock Without Hands*, was the story of an intuitive man who lived in the spacious consciousness I call Faerie time. For this man time seemed to be fluid, expanding or contracting according to his need. He would set his mind on what he wanted to accomplish and the time frame he had to work in, and he always managed to accomplish the task.

The second book, *He Lives in Two Worlds*, was the story of a man who was a medium and was comfortable relating with the spirit world as well as with his daily working life, his wife and children. It was a curious thing to receive these two books from two unknown friends, on the same day, with a similar subject. The experience moved beyond curiosity to amazement as I was rushing down the hall to get my car keys to pick up the children at school. I glanced at my watch to confirm I would be on time and saw that my trusty wristwatch no longer had its glass cover or its hands. I was wearing a clock without hands. "Something is going on here that has deep meaning," I thought, "but I just can't figure it out right now."

I see this now, 45 years later, as a prophecy of what my life would be in the future. Often I experience time as fluid, fulfilling my conscious intention to arrive someplace on time even when I didn't allow enough time for that to happen. I interact with Mano and the spirits of the land with as much comfort and ease as I relate with my family and friends. I truly do live in two worlds.

Art: A Portal of Color and Consciousness

The arts, particularly painting, are central to my work with the nature spirits, and these creative impulses entered my life in a serious way during my La Cañada years. The Council knew that art was to be a very large part of my spiritual awakening and service, so they guided me step by step to connect with my inner artist.

Art has been my healer and revealer. The healing comes in many ways. In my lack of self-consciousness, I am totally free just to paint for myself; it doesn't matter what others think or say. I am free to enjoy the process, wonder, and revelation of one color next to another. Inside of me a confidence grew over the years that I could paint something original and different. I stopped painting still life and opened to painting energies and feelings, following any pictures that revealed themselves to me. Painting gave me a way to express with color, and working and playing with color has been a lifetime passion. For me, color is an expression of God's love; it's how everything ends up coming back to God. As a child of three, I received from my mother a ream of colored paper and spent hours arranging the colors around me in patterns. When she gave me a paint set, I squeezed the paint from the tubes rather than actually putting it to paper; I wanted to experience the paint itself in all its colorful intensity. Color led me into my love for painting as an adult and allowed me to calm my worries about not drawing well.

I once was asked, "How does God show you that s/he loves you?" The answer that popped into my mind was, "Through color." Each of the seven colors of the rainbow has a specific power and gift. Angels and elementals carry the powers of each of the colors, each of the rays. When I did color healing, the colors I put on the paper opened me to receive angelic blessing, and soon, revelation.

I had always wanted to paint but could not draw like my Aunt Carolyn or Cousin Pat, so I thought I could not paint. One day I read, "If you have a strong desire to do something, God has also given you the ability." Soon, a friend enthusiastically shared the fun she was having painting with an eccentric artist. I decided to join the class, only to find that the eccentric artist had eloped with one of his students. In his place was a solid, distinguished artist, Oscar Van Name, who had stepped in to hold the class together. Oscar was not flamboyant but he was an excellent teacher. He impressed upon me that the simplicity of painting is to think in terms of using color and small shapes to build larger shapes into the finished painting. He encouraged me to keep exploring until I had the feeling: "I know I am finished." He taught me not to be afraid to over-paint and lose a picture but to trust that my first effort was just a first step: I could build more on top of it. This is the same process Mano later used to guide me in my paintings.

This concept of building a painting helped me develop my "soft eyes" expanded view and an openness to explore what wanted to emerge from the colors. Eventually I began to see gnomes in my paintings. When I looked with soft eyes, the shapes in a bowl of fruit might resemble a gnome face, or a gnome might appear in the landscape of a mountain. I wondered.

There was a time when I felt depressed, tired all of the time. With four children, my church activities, and a busy family, I found myself dragging an exhausted body around. One morning I woke up and felt and saw a hand reaching out of the heavens to take my hand and lift me. The voice said, "You can't think your way out of this. You can paint your way out." I set up a watercolor palette, fresh water brush, and a pad of paper. Each time I walked by, I put some color on the paper. The next morning I was reviewing an experience with my friend Maria. I had had energy in the morning, but after the telephone conversation with her I realized I was once again exhausted. As I was wondering about this, the inner voice said, "Resentment kills the spirit, and when the spirit dies, the body dies." I had been dragging a dead body around for weeks. With this revelation I was shown my attitude of resentment for all that I had to do, without enough time or energy to do it. I realized I had felt resentment when Maria wanted me to do something for her I felt she could do for herself.

The process I used for healing was one of observation and revelation. I observed the times when I lost my energy–after talking to Maria, for example. Then I would see a picture or get a thought about what to do next. This is the same process I use when painting from the inside. After putting color on the paper, I observe what has been going on. Then I suddenly know how to move forward: the revelation.

Another step in this painting process was how images revealed themselves as I simply put colors on the paper: gnomes, a face on the side of Half Dome, beings appearing in the shapes that made up a bowl of fruit. Angel wings and bodies appeared in loose, watery paintings. So many appeared over the years that I began to believe that these nonphysical beings were actually real and reaching out to me through my paintings. Painting has now become a communication system with Mano and Rama, my nonphysical teachers.

When I am upset, I have been guided to go to the studio, turn the sound system on loud (I usually play Beethoven's *Pastoral*), and splash color on paper. I do this until my mood shifts and I feel totally free of the upset. It is now all out on the paper in wild splashes of color. Either then or later, I often continue to paint to bring harmony or allow new pictures to appear in the mix of color and shape.

The drawing I do while sitting in meetings has revealed the energies present in the room, or the aura of a person. I used to do individual essence drawings for people at a psychic fair in San

Luis Obispo. After the energy drawing, I would interpret what the colors said to me about the person. The responses were very rewarding and encouraging and supported my knowing that I was being guided. Once I drew two 18-year-old twins. The images for one of the boys looked like outer space planets and stars; the other was a simple, quiet flow of color. The one with outer space energies said it was true; he thought constantly of the galaxy and universe. The other boy was happy hanging out in the garden in quiet spaces. My self-confidence and self-acceptance of what came out in my drawings opened me to receive the paintings Mano and Rama gave me when I moved to the Mountain and opened the Council of Gnomes.

A dear friend of mine called after visiting with me on the Mountain. She had gone back to school to get a degree in art and told me she had pondered my artwork for a long time. In essence, everything I did was "wrong" according to what she was being taught in school, but somehow I made it work. This was very similar to what Minerva Hertzhog, my dramatic, flamboyant teacher of abstract painting, had to say after I had been painting with her for two years. I had the habit of painting a red line along the nose of the face. Focusing on the nose in that way was all wrong, she said, but the outcome was interesting, so she never told me otherwise. When I started painting with Minerva I did not know Rama or Mano, but they were definitely guiding me even then.

The First Gnome

I had the message that even though it was hard, if I stayed with Minerva for at least three years, I would know everything she had to teach me. Then I was to paint at home until I knew what I needed next, before finding another teacher who could give me exactly those next steps. They also told me that it would be six months before I liked anything I did in my painting classes with Minerva.

After months of "yucko" paintings, Minerva looked at one that was dark shades of red and black and said, "Barbara, now you are going to make it. With this painting you have gotten down to your guts." And it was so; from that time things shifted, and I enjoyed the process. It was here that the gnomes started to appear. No one else really saw them, but they were clear and obvious to me, and a total wonder and mystery since I didn't believe in their reality.

Camps Farthest Out

I attended for the first time a spiritual gathering called Camps Farthest Out (CFO), and this organization was to become a vital part of my life and of my family life. The camp program was simple, and it was filled with creative expression. Each day we had singing, body movement, writing, coloring with chalk, prayer group, and morning and evening talks. The two speakers shared their lives of prayer and their personal experiences with God. With two free hours in the middle of the day, I had time to nap, integrate my experience, socialize with other campers, and walk in nature. The program was designed to move our consciousness from inner to outer and back, until at the end of the week we emerged with a whole new view of our inner and outer life, creating a balanced heart and mind.

One day in prayer group the others were praying for me but nothing was happening. The leader, who had left the room, came back, saying that Spirit had told him to return. Then I began speaking in tongues. After that, even though I didn't understand the words I was speaking in this state, I knew the feeling. Speaking in tongues opened me to a new spiritual dimension. I heard the Holy Spirit say, "I will be your teacher; don't look for other teachers." I was in the prayer group just long enough to have this opening experience. When I returned home I asked Jim, "Do I seem any different?" He said no. I replied, "Well, maybe I'm not different on the outside, but I am on the inside." I knew I had changed. I trusted Spirit now, and I had Spirit's trust.

Others Detect My Spiritual Connections

Spirit brought me three different women who could see clearly into the nonphysical world. Each one told me of the elementals she saw around me. This was interesting and mysterious to me; it was an important foreshadowing of the time when I would initiate and cultivate my own inner relationship with the nature spirits of the land.

Once while attending a spiritual retreat at a YMCA camp in the coastal redwoods of California, I was sitting on the ground in a grove of redwood trees, chatting with a friend. A very sweet feeling flowed through my heart. My friend said, "Barbara, I just saw the most amazing thing. That redwood tree leaned over and gave you a blessing." I had felt this blessing before, in meditation, and had identified it as the presence of God or the Holy Spirit. Now I began to recognize it as one of the many ways Mother Nature acknowledges and blesses me.

Another validation of connection came one night during my meditation group, when a friend with spiritual sight saw a large gnome carry two small limp, colorless, lifeless gnomes into the room and place them on the floor beside me. After a while, the little ones began to gain color, to stir and wake up. The larger, caretaker gnome later returned and took away the little ones, now bright, shiny, and lively.

A similar confirmation occurred while attending a retreat at Asilomar Conference Center on the wild and wonderful Big Sur coast near Monterey, California. Our prayer group had been sitting outside in a circle of eight or nine people, and my friend Patricia later told me that she had seen local gnomes drag seaweed from the ocean to place around me. Then they brought water elementals to sit in my aura and feel the energy of a "safe human being."

Continuing Steps Along My Destiny Path

In retrospect, I see that certain experiences during these awakening years were particularly significant in moving me toward my future tasks. At the time I wondered about them and held them in my heart, with the prayer that someday I would understand with inner certainty that "everything works together for the good for those who love God." It is very gratifying to look back and see clearly how one step led to the next in guiding me to my current place of confidence, dedication, wonder, magic, and service.

Sometimes, even early on, before I had developed my inner sight, I could sense when nature spirits were present. One Halloween, for example, I had the house decorated with corn stalks and pumpkins. I got up early to do my meditation, and as I entered the living room I became aware that the house was full of nature spirits. They were having a party. I had an unspoken knowledge that they were traveling from one location to another, stopping to rest and celebrate in inviting places where the season was being honored. They were gone by sunrise, but they filled the house with their joyous vibrant energy of fun and play.

Another playful awareness occurred in 1965, as I was driving to Indiana with the children and had what I now call an underground initiation into the daily life of a gnome community. We stopped at Carlsbad Caverns in New Mexico to stretch our legs and take a one-hour tour. As we moved from cavern to cavern, the lights turned on to welcome us into the next viewing space. Halfway through the tour we entered a room where lights shone on what appeared to be a series of small cave entrances, giving the impression of a series of stage settings. The lights showed interesting configurations of stalagmites. My vision shifted and I saw, in each lighted area, gnomes in living situations. The first was a group sitting around a dining table; another was a wedding scene. I spoke out loud to the children to tell them what I was seeing: "Look, there's a mother and child walking hand in hand; over there is a gnome family sitting on a couch and chairs, talking together." Soon the whole tour was seeing what I was seeing.

Also in 1965, I spent a week at Meadowlark Farm, a healing center in the high desert of Southern California. We had daily group meetings, private work with individual counselors, art, body movement, doctor appointments, and free time by the pool. I chose prayer and fasting as my focus for the five days. On the third day of my fast, in my inner vision, I had a "visitation." My eyes were wide open, yet it was with my inner sight that I perceived, standing in my room, a small being about a foot tall who resembled two marshmallows on top of each other. He looked at me without speaking, then began to do funny antics to get my attention. On the second visitation he took my bedroom slippers, put them on either side of his head, and said, "Look, I'm a bunny rabbit." This convinced me that I wasn't making him up but that he was his own unique being. The next day he told me I had a home within the earth, where he lived. He invited me to accompany him there. Deeply settled in my state of prayer and fasting, I had no hesitation, only total trust in God, so I said yes. I liked my house in the earth; it felt like home and I still go there. It is round with dirt walls and has a bed, table, chairs, and an artist's studio on one side of the room. I now realize that my earth home is in the realm of Faerie.

People on a spiritual path in those days often explored through guided meditation. A favorite within my group of friends was to start in an imaginal meadow, cross a river, then climb a mountain to meet a wise person on the top who was waiting to give each of us a gift. Three different times, as I followed the guidance and started up the side of the mountain, I noticed a cave off to the left with gnomes busy at work inside. Each time, I left the path leading to the wise person and entered the cave with the gnomes. Now I see that I wasn't doing something wrong; the gnomes *were* my gift, placed on my path to open my awareness and prepare me for when we would meet again and attentively work together.

During this time I also heard of Findhorn, a community in Scotland that was working consciously with angels and elementals in their garden. When Jim and I took the children to Europe in 1972, we visited Findhorn for a few days. I thought of these people as anchoring a "light of a New Age" on the planet. I wanted to walk with my family through that light and consciousness.

Fear of Nature

In 1978 I traveled to Findhorn on my own. Jim was busy with business and wasn't interested in the conference on Art and Creative Expression I wanted to attend. I had been reading of Findhorn's history of connection with the elemental spirits and angels, including R. Ogilvie Crombie's *The Gentleman and the Faun*, in which he recounts his meetings with Pan in the Edinburgh

Gnomes Call from their Cave

gardens. I routed my way back to London and Heathrow airport via a train stop in Edinburgh, with the intention of walking through the gardens myself. Maybe, just maybe, I thought, I would have an encounter with Pan.

Whatever part of my being was making these glorious plans apparently didn't connect with the part of me that was totally paralyzed with fear. My body started getting tense as the train neared Edinburgh, and my head began to ache. When I got settled in my room next to the gardens, I could hardly move or think. All I wanted to do was go to bed, and I did lie down for a while. Yet I was still determined to fulfill my mission and went off to the gardens, walked around the paths, sat on a bench, moved to another bench, all the while hurting, aching, and feeling cold. After an hour or so, I felt as if I had given it a good try. I picked up some food, returned to my room, and slept. As the train slowly moved out of Edinburgh the next morning, headed toward London and the flight home, my aching body and head relaxed. One part of me was sorry I had not met Pan; another part was delighted.

Verification of a New Seeing

In 1983, I finally became a believer. Driving on Highway 5 near Coalinga, I saw a huge gnome shape in a smokestack off in the distance. I asked my Aunt Katherine what she saw in that smokestack. "It's a gnome, Barbara," she replied. This was the first time someone had verified what I was seeing. It gave me confidence to believe that, indeed, a gnome was connecting with me—that what was going on inside and around me was real.

SAN LUIS OBISPO YEARS

"HEED THE SIGNS ALONG THE HIGHWAY." This statement floated through my mind the day Jim called to say he was quitting his job and wanted to move to a community with clean air. In the previous three years, both Maria and Patricia had been telling me they saw that I was going to move away from La Cañada. Stunned to think the time had come, I went upstairs to lie down. The doorbell rang and when I returned the door was open, but no one was there. At that moment the phone rang. It was Maria, telling me that Gene Dorsey, my first spiritual teacher, had just come to her and wanted to speak to me. I sat down, got quiet, put my attention in my heart, and sent Gene love. I felt his presence and said, "I have not been aware of you since you died." He responded that his work had taken him to other dimensions but that he was always aware of my light. He had seen my light flare, knew that I needed support, and immediately came. He encouraged me, saying, "This move will open many doors and you will love what happens and who you become." I had never had anything like this happen before, yet the whole experience felt comforting and natural. I was filled with a sense of awe at the easy connection between worlds, and also was filled with deep gratitude to know that on some level, Gene was watching over me. "Heeding the signs along the highway'" became a continuing trusted guidance.

When we began to think where we would move, Jim expressed his desire to live in a small community with clean air. As a real estate appraiser he needed to be in a county seat so he could conveniently look up property records. I thought of our last family vacation, which had started with a night at the Madonna Inn in San Luis Obispo. As we walked toward the car in the morning, we were stunned to see a beautiful, bright double rainbow covering the whole expanse of the city and valley. I remembered thinking at the time, "This has a special significance." It was another sign along the highway. San Luis Obispo was the first location we explored, and it turned out to be an easy and excellent choice. In our home there we created a garden, planted fruit trees, and acquired a horse, goats, and chickens. I learned to spin goat hair into yarn for weaving fabric that I then made into stoles, ponchos, coats, and jackets. Each week I made goat cheese. We had such an abundance of milk, I joked that I could finally understand how Cleopatra was able to bathe in milk. I now say that the Council moved us to the country so I could relate more intimately with nature. This allowed me to homestead, get my hands into the dirt, watch seeds grow into carrots, beans, and corn. I also learned to can the foods that we grew. Jim's training in the garden included a weeding session in which he mistook the baby carrots for weeds and pulled them right out.

The day we moved from La Cañada, as the moving van pulled out of the driveway, Jim realized that the key to the car was in the desk drawer—on the van. The phone rang. It was my friend Patricia, who said, "What is going on? The elementals of your land and the angels of the mountain are very upset. Something is happening, and they don't understand." When I told her we were moving, she suggested, "Talk to them, tell them what is going on. Release them from your service and prepare them for the next owners." We had a sweet conversation with the elementals, filled with gratitude, love, and release. Some didn't want to part from the family and asked to come with us; of course I said yes. Thirty years later, I returned to that house we had designed and where we raised our four children. When the lady of the house opened the door, I was flooded with the joy and loving, exuberant recognition from the angels and elementals of the house and land.

I realize now that beings on the Council have always been aware of what was going on in my life. They have given me promptings, dreams, and intuitions to guide my thinking. It has always been my choice whether to heed these signs and change my course of action, or to plow through on my own and learn from experience. I see this learning as one more way I was being guided to people who work consciously with the nonphysical intelligence of nature. My human teachers have often been friends who possessed knowledge that I was seeking and for which I was ready. Typically, I would have two primary friends I was learning from spiritually, and they would totally disagree with each other. This happened over and over, and I think it served to open my mind and heart to the multi-dimensionality in which Spirit works. In this way I was encouraged to find my own path, and I took to using oracles and divination practices to guide me along the way.

Practical Assistance

Around this time, while we were living in San Luis Obispo, I got into the habit of calling on Faerie beings to help me thread my needles and open the plugged hole in my pierced ear, of asking for traffic lights to turn green and parking places to appear close to my destination. I don't know how they do it, but they fulfill my requests more often than not.

Once I asked for a parking place near my destination. It was not there and I had to park and walk two blocks. It was a pleasant day and I was not in a hurry, but I wondered, and asked Spirit why there had not been a place in front of the art store. The inner voice responded, telling me they had called on me to be of service. I was wearing a bright rose-pink dress. A woman sitting in the window of a restaurant was deeply depressed, and as she looked out the window and saw the color of my dress, the color angels imparted the rose-pink ray into her heart and gave her blessings and release.

I have also had great success asking the nature spirits to help me find things I have lost. They told me to stop yammering "help me, help me" and to take action. It was easier for them, they said, if I visualized the object in my mind, then started creating order by putting things away. "It is easier to direct a moving stone than a stationary one; when you are in movement we are able to guide you to the lost item." My children have heard this many times. Once when my son had lost his car keys and I reminded him of the process, he said, "Oh Mom, you just tell me that so I will clean up my room." He came back in one minute; he'd found the keys under the first thing he picked up.

Vision Quest to Europe, 1984 - Returning to Findhorn

Two months after seeing the gnome in the smokestack and having Aunt Katherine confirm that she also saw the image, Jim and I left on our year-long journey to Europe to explore how God would use our time and talents as individuals and

as a couple. Our children were grown by this time, and we were committed to clarifying and rededicating our internal and external work.

We started this adventure with three months at the Findhorn Foundation in Scotland. The prerequisite to participating in a program is to attend an

Barbara & Jim in Berlin

Experience Week, in which a Findhorn facilitator introduces guests to various aspects of the community such as spirit, relationship, finances, and nature. Because I had already done this, while Jim was attending I went to the Isle of Iona, off the coast of Scotland.

It was a wild, windy week on the island. When I arrived, I spoke to the lady at the grocery store and she told me both of the hotels were closed for the winter. The ferry had gone for the day. She didn't know of any place for me to stay; all of the rooms she rented in season were now being renovated. She decided she could let me have one room but no kitchen or sitting area. With a grateful heart, I said yes. Cooking my meals in an electric teapot was a great adventure: boiled potatoes and carrots, Ovaltine (a childhood favorite I had not had for years), tea, instant soup, instant oatmeal. It all worked fine, though cleaning the teakettle was a challenge.

Someone had given me *The Mists of Avalon* to read, a feminine version of the King Arthur story. I had never heard of a Mother God. In my basic Christian background, I had developed a sweet loving relationship with my Father God, and I didn't like changing my belief structure. I didn't want to expand to something new. However, this was the only available reading material, so I sat on the bed in my room and read it. At the end of my week, sitting on a bench looking at the splashing waves and stormy sky, I had the awareness that this vision quest was going to take my familiar belief structure gently apart, spread it out before me, then reassemble it in a new way a year later, when I was ready to return home.

During our three months at Findhorn, we participated in a program called the Essence of Findhorn, with the purpose of creating a small community within the larger Findhorn community. Twelve people gathered from eight different countries. Jim and

Standing Stones

I were the only couple and the oldest in the group. We each chose a work crew to be part of for the three months. I decided to work in the garden at Cluny Hill Hotel, the home of a few community residents and most of the guests who came week by week to participate in various Findhorn pro-grams. This, I see now, was a major step in my coming into the embrace of Mother Earth. Each morning my garden department created a circle by holding hands and attuning to the angel of the garden. We chose the jobs we would do that day and gathered up tools, always mindful that tools, too, are a form of consciousness and worthy of being named.

Following the English tradition, we stopped for tea twice a day. Freshly baked bread, Ryvita, peanut butter and jelly were always available along with the tea. When we finished working for the day we would clean the tools, thanking them for their work, put them back in their places, and again hold hands in a circle to release the garden angels and give thanks for the work accomplished.

In the last week of our stay at Findhorn, my job of moving small cactus plants from a sand tray to a pot gave me a new experience. I received a clear message to be careful. The cactus I was about to move had long white feathery spines. I took two spoons and placed one on each side of the plant, to be careful and protect myself as I moved it to the pot. The residential gardener came to see how the work was unfolding. She looked at the little cactus and said, "Oh look, this one is crying." On each side, where I had held it with the spoons, the flesh was broken and liquid was seeping out. I had a flash of awareness that the little plant had been telling me to be careful with her. I realized her long white spines were Mother Nature's way of protecting her tender flesh, and I saw one more way to practice looking beyond my own reality.

Honoring Neolithic Stones

Mother Nature guided me to organize the next part of our trip around visits to the Neolithic stone monuments, stone circles, and cairns dotted all over England, Wales, and Scotland—even though at that time I had no understanding of their significance. I could tell, however, that each one had a definite and individual feeling. Jim and I took small faceted crystals and buried one at each site, with a prayer to release any trapped spirits, and to heal all the painful memories that spirits, people, and souls might be holding from living or even visiting there, or perhaps from doing ritual. We visualized each crystal as holding the consciousness of the Christ, and the colors within the crystals represented color rays and color angels.

Now I see that this Neolithic safari was also flowing along with Mano's guidance of my initiation into service to Mother Earth—

coming directly on the heels of my initial and true meeting with her while working in the Findhorn garden. It also involved a Neolithic call to connect with my past lives in those sacred places.

Once on a damp day while visiting the Merry Maidens in Cornwall, I stood in the center, closed my eyes, and prayed to the guardian of the site. I felt a warm energy beside me and was excited to have made connection. When I opened my eyes, I found a huge cow there rather than the spirit I had been expecting. She may have been a guardian cow, but nevertheless she brought me a lesson on staying open and flexible.

Traveling Freely

We visited people, attended conferences, and explored international communities. When people found I had lived at Findhorn most everyone asked what it was like. My answer was always the same: "I experienced winter, with sunrise at 9 am and sunset at 4. All day felt magical, with beautiful colors in the clouds like twilight. I worked in the garden." Every time I said that I had worked in the garden I started to cry, tears rolling down my cheeks, my voice choked. I felt my heart deepen. It took many months for me to realize that working in the Findhorn garden five days a week for three months had been my meeting with Mother Nature. Now she was em-bracing me in her love and moving me to tears.

Manor House B&B

Jim wanted to attend a peace conference in Holland, and to fill the time before it began we signed up for a week-long training of circle dance teachers in Glastonbury, England, the home of King Arthur, the mystical Tor, and the lovely Chalice Well—definitely a magical place. We stayed at a B&B on the side of Chalice Hill in a lovely ancient manor house. This became our home away from home, where we returned often between destinations. This week of circle dancing from 10 to 5 each day nearly fried my brain. Some people dance with their bodies, knowing exactly what to do once the step has been explained. I discovered that I dance in my head, and by the end of the week my brain was tired and I could not add or read. This "fried brain" took me into an altered state and sometimes, when sitting on the floor in a circle with the other dancers, my vision would shift and I would see one man turn into a gnome. Later it seemed another example of

my Council training me to perceive its reality. The circle dance training also prefigured the many years of sacred circle dancing in the Amphitheater, a beloved time of community building and touching-in-with-spirit.

One day while driving through a small village in England, I casually glanced in the store windows as we passed. My eye caught something in an antique shop and the inner prompting said to stop and look. It was a

Angels, Elementals & Humans

small ivory screen, created when people lived by candlelight and women covered blemishes on their faces with wax. The screen was to keep the candlelight from melting the wax. The carving was a delicate, detailed image of an angel floating above a city and carrying a child in her arms. We bought it to celebrate my upcoming birthday, and it still sits in my living room with a light behind it as a constant call and prayer for angels to take care of the little ones in the world.

During this year of traveling, I established a communication with the angels after noticing a tiny white pinfeather floating through the air or onto a bench I was about to sit on. For a while I only noticed and wondered, then I finally recognized that angels were actually communicating with me. Once as I got into the car I saw two pinfeathers on the roof...and was surprised to see them still there when we reached our destination. This angelic connection became a constant comfort and support as we traveled.

The day after we returned home, our year-old granddaughter went to the emergency hospital, having fallen on asphalt from the second story of her home. On my way to the hospital, I went to the Amphitheater and said aloud, "I can't stay long. I just wanted you to know what is happening to Suzanne. Please help her." At that moment I noticed what looked like a leaf floating from the top of the madrone tree on the other side of the Amphitheater, gently, gently, gently floating toward me. As it got close I saw that it was a small white pinfeather. I put out my hand and it landed in my palm. I knew the angels were there and that my granddaughter would survive. She did, and now is an adult with a beautiful family of her own.

All through the trip I pondered the reality of angels and elementals. I carried a knowing and not-knowing conflicting energy within me. I had many visions of angels and started making drawings of the angel energy in the cities we visited. It was a constant push-pull between my heart that wanted to believe, and my mind that didn't want to be wrong. Two things happened during the last week of our trip to help resolve this dilemma. While visiting the London Museum, I saw statues from ancient times of animals with wings. Looking at them, I felt peace flowing through my heart and mind. The ancient people clearly knew of angels; therefore, angels must be real. On our last night in England we stayed one final time at the Chalice Well Guest House in Glastonbury. I read in the founder Wesley Tudor Pole's diary, "When the planet was first inhabited, angels, elementals, and humans worked harmoniously together." That did it; my mind was finally at peace.

In the beginning humans knew and worked harmoniously with both the angelic and elemental kingdoms. Somehow, somewhere along the way, we humans became separated from this original knowledge. The prophecy I felt on Iona in my first week of our journey was fulfilled. All of the pieces of my belief structure had been pulled apart and put back together, and now I was very comfortable with the thought that God is Mother as well as Father. Now I can easily say, "Yes, Barbara, angels and elementals are real." With that clarity, my heart was also at peace.

Upon our return, after a short stay in Santa Cruz, we went home to San Luis Obispo. As we drove into our valley, we stopped to say hello to a neighbor who was taking a walk on the road. I looked over at our home nestled into the foot of a rocky cliff and saw the shapes of the rock take the form of a gnome standing tall, with hat, jacket, and boots. When I told Jim and our neighbor what I was seeing, neither of them could see it. I accepted this as being my personal welcome from the gnomes on the mountain. It was comforting to realize I no longer needed someone else to confirm what I saw.

TRANSITION TO THE MOUNTAIN & BEN LOMOND

I ALWAYS HAD AN INNER FEELING that my home base was in the redwoods of Northern California. Before we started out on our European pilgrimage, an unusual opportunity had come up to buy a piece of land we knew and loved near Santa Cruz. The first time I visited this land was when my friend Dorothy Olson took me there to see the Amphitheater and meet her friend Kay Ortmans and others. However, when we got to the point of actually visiting the Amphitheater, just as we were starting down the stairs, Dorothy looked at her watch and said, "Oh Barbara, we don't have time to go down." Standing at the top of the stairway, I could feel a powerful and gentle energy floating up to greet me. I was filled with spirit and a spontaneous song came floating out. Sad and disappointed, I walked with Dorothy to our car and the next destination.

At the time, Jim and I were living in La Cañada and had been dreaming of having a little place in the redwoods. I had heard of a new way to pray by visualizing what you want, holding it with love for a few days, then letting it go. Stimulated by the feeling of the Amphitheater, I followed the prayer guidance, saying that I wanted to own property like the Amphitheater. Ten years later, while attending a CFO camp in the redwoods north of Santa Cruz, Dorothy's daughter Denby came to camp for the day. When she saw me, she came running over and said, "Oh Barbara, they are going to sell the Amphitheater and we will never get to use it again." Within my heart, Spirit said, "Buy it." I called Jim to see if we had enough money, and he was as excited as I was. I put a down payment on it the next day and escrow was closed the following week—August 9, 1983, on my birthday. I knew I was coming home at last. Years later Mano told me he had put out a call, and when I stood at the top of the stairs and sang that song, he knew I had accepted. With this he started setting up arrangements for me to be able to purchase the Amphitheater, those many years later.

Another affirmation came one morning at the ranch, while I was sitting outside watching the dawn arrive. I heard the inner voice say, "Barbara, I do not need you in San Luis Obispo any longer. I need you on the Mountain." Jim and I put our house up for sale the next day in preparation for the move to the Santa Cruz Mountains. Now we were ready to begin our collaboration in an active, true way. I loved our house in San Luis Obispo. It was a cross between a farmhouse and mountain lodge, designed by a wonderful architect. One large room had nooks and crannies, lofts for beds, a loom, a sun porch for passive solar, and a wood burning stove in front of a three-quarter-tall stone wall

Our San Luis Obispo Home

in the middle of the big room. However, when Spirit said she needed me on the Mountain, it was easy to release that which I loved, knowing I would also love where I was being called.

Buying Hanna & Barney Smead's Cabin, 1983

Jim told me that Hanna and Barney were going to sell their cabin and he would like to buy it. Others had wanted to buy it but Hanna refused, saying they were too worldly. I felt cautious; I was in the process of designing a house and studio on Hill Top. My plan was to build the studio right away to have a place to stay when we came to the Amphitheater, then build the house when we actually planned to move to the Mountain. To please Jim, I said I would look at the cabin, but I had a closed mind. I was afraid I would get stuck living there.

Hanna showed me through the rooms. Every room was draped off to keep the heat focused in the kitchen/living area. I could see that the roof had nice lines and the rooms were open and comfortable. I decided to agree, thinking we could use it now and rent it to "like-minded people" when we moved to the new house on Hill Top.

Hanna was known as a "Prayer Warrior," living deep in her faith. She and Barney prayed daily for the Second Coming of Christ and offered their little cabin as refuge for the Amphitheater angels to live during the months the Rajneesh devotees were living in the Amphitheater. The day we told Hanna we wanted to buy the cabin, she said, "I know. The Lord told me, 'Hanna, this lady does not think like you but she is also my woman, and this is to be her home.'"

It took more than a year for our San Luis Obispo house to sell; in the meantime, we focused on creating a cottage out of the cabin. I experienced the cabin as charming but pure funk, cold and dark, with no closets and no room large enough to hold our queen-sized bed. Jim was charmed by the fireplace made from a 50-gallon drum on its side—that is, until it filled the house with smoke but no heat.

When we came back from our year In Europe, I had lived in so many old houses that I was used to "funky charm". On that trip I became concerned for Mother Earth, as I saw so much open land being covered with houses and cement. Spirit kept dropping ideas into my mind on ways to make the cabin comfortable and livable. With that clear guidance, Jim and I moved into the grand adventure of creating a cottage out of the little mountain cabin.

We had hired a contractor to help us with the cabin's transformation. Barney was quite proud of his little cabin, which had started as a large tent. When God gave him windows and doors from the dump, he said he knew it was time to add more substance and structure to it. I say God gave us Barney's cabin and from it we created a charming cottage. We added a fireplace for heat, skylights for daytime vision, and closets. We pushed a front window out to make room for an oven and built an annex to the bedroom to make it large enough for our bed. Going for peasant charm, I painted flowers around the inner fascia board in the kitchen, eating, and sitting areas.

I had lived in this cottage and loved it for more than 15 years when one day I had a flash memory of visiting Hanna 20 years earlier. As I watched her put food away in her kitchen, I had had a clear knowing that in my elder years I would be putting groceries away in that same kitchen.

Our Ben Lomond Home

Meeting Mano

PART TWO

MEETING MANO,
LEARNING TO TRUST

1987–2000

MY TWO PRIMARY TEACHERS

IN 30 YEARS OF LIVING ON THE MOUNTAIN in the heart of a redwood forest, I have walked to the Amphitheater more than 7,000 times. The Amphitheater is a large open space surrounded by mature madrone and redwood trees, a sacred portal of entry to the Spirit world. I am often aware of elemental and angelic energies there and have learned to identify and relate with a number of them. Two major spirit teachers work with me to help me understand my experiences and teach me about nature and the world of Faerie. Rama is an angel, of whom I have been aware since the 1970s; Mano is a gnome.

The Angel Rama

During the time in La Cañada when I became acquainted with a number of healers and teachers, I worked with Olivia Crawford, a psychic who told me that my teacher wanted to connect with me. She integrated Rama into me, and he has watched over me all along. As my over-guiding angel, Rama supported me when I first met Mano: "This is right; this is good," he would assure me, "you have nothing to fear." He is my stable base of consciousness, and I associate him with my higher Self.

The Gnome Mano

The first day on the mountain I was filled with excitement. After half a day of unpacking I wanted to go to the Amphitheater to connect with whoever had inspired this move by saying, "Barbara, I don't need you in San Luis Obispo any longer. I need you on the Mountain." I felt the answer to the mystery was in the Amphitheater. On this cool October morning, I put on a down jacket, hat, and scarf and walked down to pay my respects. I felt a presence walking beside me. Looking with my inner eye I saw a large gnome, my same height, 5'6". This was a new experience for me, yet still I felt comfortable. He didn't say hello or introduce himself. He just started teaching me something about time and space being flexible and nothing being set solid. Recently he has reminded me that in this first direct teaching he told me, "Time is not governed by the hands on the clock. Time is governed by segments of intention." That first day when I entered the Amphitheater, the arrangement of the chairs gave me the feeling that invisible beings were in council. I felt the presence of the land and felt loved and welcomed.

Mano works with and for the gods that serve Mother Earth in the Amphitheater. His challenge in relationship to me was, first, to inspire my move to the Mountain, and then to interest me in coming to the Amphitheater regularly. He urged me to come at 10:00 every morning to paint, using this space as my studio until mine was built (in 1989). Each morning he was there to greet me. Painting was very important to me by this time, and Mano introduced me to the idea of painting the energies of nature, of the Amphitheater itself, the spirits of the land, and the angels.

LEARNING TO SEE & COMMUNICATE

AS I OPENED MY HEART TO MANO, I realized that I had seen him twice before. The first time he appeared as the large gnome in the smokestack when I was driving with Aunt Katherine. The second was the day we returned from our year in Europe and I looked up at Indian Knob, the outcropping of rocks above our

San Luis Obispo home, and saw the imprint of a large gnome welcoming us.

Recently Mano has described three different ways I have learned to see him and the other spirit beings with whom I interact. The "inside me" seeing is more a feeling but also contains vision. I have named this see/feel, and it is my basic way of discerning spirit beings. Mano first spoke to me in this modality the day I moved to the Mountain and he walked beside me. The "outside of me" seeing comes through my outer vision. Mano has shown himself to me only twice in this manner, both during my first year on the Mountain. Once he appeared in my living room. I could see his black boots on the floor and his blue jacket and red cap touching the ceiling. He was transparent, not solid—I could see through him—and I think I was perceiving the subtle realm of the physical.

Both times I was with someone who was acquainted with elementals. The first was Brooks, my friend from La Cañada, who had an elemental companion named o den du. The second was Colin Harrison, who led a week-long circle dance workshop. On the last day of the workshop, so tired I couldn't think, I looked at Colin across the room and saw him as a gnome. The combination of my friends' fairy energy and my own helped me see these elementals. The third seeing Mano identified is "overshadowing and transforming a physical substance." This happened the day I saw Mano's image in the smokestack when I was driving.

I have witnessed a fourth way but have never experienced it myself. My friend Maria, of Panamanian and Chinese heritage, has had spiritual sight from birth. She often sees beings in the subtle world as physical. As a child she could not tell the difference, and her mother accused her of lying. As an adult she learned to discern the difference, though the subtle beings look as physical as humans.

I have at times been critical of the "cutesy" way I see others depicting elementals—the great god Pan being reduced to Peter Pan, for example, or acquaintances spotting unicorns and colorful fairies peeking out from behind trees. When I have asked Mano and Rama about what seem to me to be superficial encounters, they calm me down and open me up. "You have your way," they say, "others have theirs. You can only share what is true for you and refrain from making them wrong for what is true for them. You have a highly developed mental side in balance with a mature feeling side of life; you see things with mental, heartful clarity. It is just one approach. There is no right or wrong. Spirit will use any 'hook' to move people into relating, sharing their stories, and waking others to the reality of the consciousness within nature."

I received greater confidence in the truth of these different realms of being when reading *Summer with the Leprechauns* by Tanis Helliwell. Having rented a cottage in the west of Ireland for the summer, Helliwell, with her psychic vision, met a leprechaun who told her he had been assigned to relate with her. He said that many years earlier, a man in a dark coat had come into the inner realm of nature looking for volunteers to work with humans. When I read that the man was Rudolf Steiner, everything in my heart relaxed and fell into place; I thought, Oh, what I am doing is really true. I also carried the memory from the end of my year's visioning journey with Jim: Tudor Pole's diary stated that in the beginning, angels, elementals, and humans worked together to inhabit the planet. Mano brought to me the urgency of reestablishing this connection.

When I asked to get to know the beings of my land, I was told that I would not see them with my physical eyes; I would see them in my imagination. I would see them through my heart by feeling their presence. They told me, "Your presence in the Amphitheater is always a sign of celebration. You are becoming more attuned to our energies and it is easier now to connect and speak with you."

How Spirit Beings Manifest

The elementals help me discern the presence of spiritual beings around me through nature's four elements.

- *Spirit presences rise from the realm of earth.* I may hear a snap in the wall, a creak of the ceiling. Mano described it as a spirit breaking the sound barrier, with a responding outer-world noise.

- *They signal through water.* Water expresses itself through feeling, a feeling of presence, of *yes* or *no*.

Air Elemental

- *They come through the air.* I feel a breeze on my face when the windows are all closed. Outside, one leaf on a plant next to me swings and wiggles with frantic joy though the rest of the leaves are quiet. I have the feeling that an elemental spirit is jumping on the leaf. A deep involuntary breath (which I document in my notes as .db) tells me that the angels and my presence are in agreement with the thought I have just expressed or heard. It is a significant confirmation of truth.

- *They express themselves in fire.* In the presence of fire, when truth is spoken a flash and rush of heat goes through my body and my face gets red. Little sparkly lights zip around in front of me. The flame of a candle might flare as high as four inches or flicker up and down when a fire spirit wants to interact with me.

Communication Protocol

After working for some time on Mano's suggestions for communicating, I devised this protocol to guide my memory.

1. Be clear about the being you want to dialogue with. Create a sacred space. I do this with an alignment chant to still time, space, and motion.

2. Create a bridge from outer to inner. Visualize a setting. Open your heart for connection.

3. Name what you want to dialogue about. Be specific. This will help you focus and will help Spirit know what you want. Out of a 360-degree possibility, at what degree are you asking to meet?

4. Prime the pump. Tell what is going on for you.

5. Notice how dialogue begins. For me, the "second voice" takes up my thinking with new awareness, insight, and information. If this doesn't happen right away, I ask a specific question. The answer may come with a feeling of yes or no.

6. If the dialogue still doesn't start, close the session. Don't hang around trying to make it happen. Tell your partner that you will come back again. Set a time. Ask: Is there any way I can make this easier for you?

7. Determine a specific way to close the session, to release the energies holding sacred space. The opening creates a segment in time, set aside from normal time, to interact with the timeless dimension. Having a formal closing prevents the energy from leaking out.

8. Express gratitude. Remember that in this process you are in kindergarten, if not preschool.

The Computer as a Communication Tool

Each day as I enter the grove, I lean into a beautiful redwood tree I call the Mother. One day I heard her say, "Tomorrow, bring your laptop computer, sit on the ground with your back to my trunk, visualize Mano in front of you, and write what you hear." When I was finished, she said, "Now do this each morning until you leave for Europe." I came every morning for the next three months. Most often, Mano would make this request: "Speak to us. Greet us. Tell us you appreciate the beauty we offer you." This was the beginning of my adventure as a recorder of elemental messages. I have more than 600 pages of keyboarded messages. When I returned from that trip and met Mano in the Amphitheater, he asked me to take my computer to my studio and "open Council". I followed his instructions and have continued to do so each time I go to the studio to paint. That was the beginning of my awareness of the Council of Gnomes, which had been waiting since my birth for this connection.

By using my laptop, I have a record and can go back to learn and ask other questions. Because I have to move into another part of my mind to dialogue, it is easy to forget what was said. I do this recording in nature, with my back to a tree, or in my studio. Another person I know does it in the house, sitting by his favorite houseplant. My process is now well established, so I can make contact anywhere, just by setting up sacred space and opening to the connection.

Talking with Mano

I experience the elementals' communication as being extremely subtle. When I tell you, "a gnome spoke to me," it sounds very solid and real, and you might think, "I wish I could hear so clearly." It is really not that loud and clear. I have simply learned to accept the fleeting thoughts and to follow the threads that lead me. I have learned to trust myself to write the thoughts as they come. If I stop as I write to question and wonder, I move from intuition and inspiration to my intellect, and the whole creative flow is aborted. The computer helps me keep this flow moving. "There is subliminal teaching going on all of the time," Mano has told me. "You pick it up and translate it into words. Speak to us and look for us often during the day. Take us as constant companions. The more you remember to talk with us, the closer and clearer our work will become."

The Heart Center

"The thing I want to address is your heart energy," Mano told me early on, "the presence of your awareness centered in your heart. As you develop this centering habit, you will find yourself feeling more nourished and attuned to plants and persons around you. Nature speaks through the heart; the only way you can 'hear' Spirit is through your heart. We want you to focus on the heart, then keep your awareness open to the larger field of presence. I realize that you feel as if you have been working with this energy for a long time. It is so. And what I want you to realize is that you have achieved great success in your heart attunement. You would not be talking to me now if that were not so."

Expect an Answer

The first request ever made of me, and the one I think I have heard most often, is simply to say hello. Hello to the plants, hello to Mother Nature, hello to wind and rain–to send love to all of nature around me and consciously be aware of receiving the love nature sends back. The first time I did this with true awareness, I walked to the Amphitheater touching each plant and saying "Hello, I love you." By the time I had finished the seven-minute walk, I was giddy with joy and filled with a sense of total wellbeing. My intimate offering to touch, send love, and greet nature was received and given back to me one thousand-fold.

Mano continually reinforces this simple exchange: "Perfect protocol when relating with nature spirits is to say hello and thank you. This opens your consciousness and heart to their presence. From that point, many things can happen. Notice what impresses your consciousness: What do you see, sense, feel, or hear? There are many ways to relate and co-create in friendship with a gnome. You can learn a great deal about the physical body, what foods to eat, the weather, growth of plants. Always ask, 'How can I serve you? What do you want me to know?'" The other reminder I receive often is that when I first step outside and feel the fresh air, I am to receive it as a blessing and to think of it as receiving Mother Nature's Darshan, the blessing from a Holy One. By following this guidance, my inner vision became clearer and my confidence grew through repeated experiences.

"When possible," the gnomes tell me, "have your feet on the soil as you walk. When on concrete, see your feet going beneath, to the surface of the earth. Send love through your feet to the earth and through your eyes to all of nature around you. Then become conscious of the energy coming back to you. As you walk the earth, enrich your experience by sending blessings. See your feet radiating love into the earth with every step, leaving footprints of love and light wherever you go. Each city, village, park, forest, or special place in nature has its own over-lighting nature intelligence, its own guardian deity, called by some the Genii Loci. Breathe the air consciously and with gratitude. Speak to the angels and elementals of that place. Ask how you can assist them and how they can assist you. Speak to the plants as you walk; touch them, tell them they are beautiful. Speaking and expecting an answer is of enormous assistance in helping the nature spirits relate with a conscious human being. This does not happen very often; some of us are falling asleep from lack of interaction."

They remind me to trust my inner visions and feelings of the subtle world I live within. "When you see a face in the bark or leaves of a tree, open your heart and say *hello*. Ask if it wants to speak to you. Ask what you can do for it." Once, while sitting in the car waiting for Jim, I spoke to a face I saw in a tree. The elemental said he was an elf. He was so excited to be talking with a human, he ran to get other elves to come and see for themselves and participate in the experience.

A special order of hardy nature spirits has volunteered to serve the plantings along the freeways and in the heart of cities. I have been asked to send them love and appreciation, to speak to them and touch them if I am close enough. This encourages them and makes their work easier, knowing they are recognized and appreciated, not simply taken for granted.

Hardy Nature Spirit

Exuberance and Passion

One day as I walked to the Amphitheater I heard Mano say, "You were an exuberant child raised in a household of repressed adults." Looking within, I could see the truth I had never realized before. I wanted to be free to express that exuberance, that passion for life, the joy and delight in the mysteries Mano was revealing to me. It didn't happen all at once. I had to deal with the fear of being "too much" for people. This dilemma resolved when, talking with a friend, I realized: I have a good heart. I am not showing off or trying to impress people. Then an inner knowing floated to the surface, saying, "I can totally trust the fullness of who I AM." With that new level of trust and freedom, I have set my spirit free to respond to my intuitions, follow promptings, allow and totally enjoy my heart's opening to wider vistas in both my inner and outer life. It has made me wonder, though, how often adults' worries and teachings repress and dampen children's passions and exuberance.

Exuberant Child

The elementals encourage me to mix my serious dedication with exuberance. They want the energies recorded in my writing to come through the filter of joy as well as love–in order to keep the love "bright and sparkling". "I have been watching you over the years," a small sprightly fairy told me once. "I've seen you in the Amphitheater and going here and there, and I am always surprised that you are so serious about what you do. I see beneath the serious coat a dancing, bubbly, effervescent energy. The serious coat dampens the light you carry and holds in, contains, the nourishment that you could interchange with us. We watch each day to see if that joy is going to be released so we can participate with it." I thanked the fairy for coming and asked for help in freeing the joy. "There is nothing we can't do for you," the fairy responded. "We can dance around you, lift your experience, and invite you to join us in the dance. As you say *yes*, I can see things beginning to break loose." When I asked the fairy's name, she identified herself as Joy. "I ride on the back of the hummingbird that comes close to look at you. I belong to these mountains, to the Amphitheater.

I have watched you for years and have asked to speak to you."

I know that the nature spirits welcome my passion. One foggy day, for example, they told me: "You need this moisture in the air, as it feeds the emotional and etheric bodies. To maintain balance and wholeness, we want to connect with you through your feelings as well as through mental telepathy. The Hawaiian music you have been listening to nourishes these feelings. It has that lush warm misty energy that we need for you and from you. Some call it passion. When passion is expressed solely within the mind, it is powerful and intense. When it comes from the heart and body, it is nourishing and strengthening. We are asking you to bring this heart energy to the nature spirits on your land. Send love and speak to the nature spirits within each green and growing plant. In the beginning this nourishment, warmth, and interactive affection was always present between human and nature. Since the burning times it has been missing. We need it now."

The nature spirits remind me to "Live life abundantly in relation-ship with nature, recognizing the elemental beings and angels when you feel the freshness of ocean, lake, stream, rain, or snow. Be aware of the elemental consciousness within the water you drink, the water you wash in, when you feel the warmth of the sun. Take time to rejoice in the beauty the color angels create to herald dawn and dusk with sunrise and sunset. Be aware of the seasons and live vibrantly with gratitude for Mother Nature's bounty, the generosity and beauty of each season. Savor the flavor of cherries in spring, watermelon in summer, apples in autumn. Enjoy the first bulbs of spring, the leaves that turn in the fall, the winter storm, and summer vacation. For all of your conscious relating with us, we give you the gift of a grateful heart."

Mano adds, "Much is being asked of humans and of nature. Since the Christ energy has entered the heart of the planet (December 22, 2012) and as we move into the next age, we are all receiving an enormous jolt of energy. When we work together and share our love and passion, it is much easier to carry this increased light frequency with balance and wholeness."

The nature beings have always appeared to me as gnomes. They actually may be something else, but this was the easiest way for me to identify them with the earth and with nature. Early in my connection Mano reminded me, "We are not sprightly little men and women. We are wizards who can shape-shift as needed to work in any dimension we are called to serve. We are a light substance, a consciousness within the earth herself." My understanding is that they can take on whatever shape and form is needed in order to do a certain work or become recognizable to a particular human. I once read that basically a nature being lives in its "light body" and only takes a form when it wants to connect with a person. The angels don't need wings; the gnomes don't really have red hats. I think of angel wings and red gnome hats simply as "calling cards".

LEVELS OF GNOMES & EARTH SPIRITS

"THERE ARE MANY ORDERS OF GNOMES and earth spirits who interact with humans, and many levels of consciousness among us," Mano has told me. "Some humans, in indigenous cultures for example, are especially sensitive to the nonphysical world. These original people share a conscious giving and receiving with the earth elementals." For me he advised, "Keep refining the identity of your gnome Council. Each refinement is a jog in your memory to what was true in earlier times and what is now taking place again. Your team includes three categories of gnomes: masters, teachers, and workers or companions. We are in an evolutionary pattern of growth in the same manner as humans. We have different names for each degree of gnome consciousness. For you, the one word, 'gnome', is enough to identify us as earth beings. We are your team and your Council, your workers, partners, and friends. We have been with you from the beginning of time, and we, like you, are part of the God-self."

Master Gnomes

According to Mano, "Deep within the interior structure of earth are the master gnomes. These beings work with the laws of the universe, moving energies to keep the balance of earth in relationship to the movement of moon, sun, planets, and stars. The master gnomes are working to help Mother Earth move into a higher vibration than she presently holds. To do this, her protégé, humanity, must also move into a higher frequency. It is closely watched and deeply desired for humans to relate with earth spirits."

When I asked Mano if he is a master gnome, he replied: "That is not a term I would use for myself, though all who work with you are in some ways at the master level. I am the overseer of this project. I am in charge of the process of calling you and other humans out of your stupor of unconsciousness and back into your soul-knowing of earth wisdom and mystery. You might say I am the master of the mystery. I wait for your attention. Your requests for help are often shuttled over to my office. You think you are asking the angels and often that request comes to me. It would be in order for you to call on me directly."

Teacher Gnomes

Mano is clearly my major teacher. When I asked for specific ways to work with him, he replied, "When you see a need in nature, when you are aware of people with body ailments, body limitations, organizations that are not working well, you can call on me and my office of interacting with humans and of perfecting nature's form. I realize that these may sound very different, but they are much the same. One is a form in the natural world, the other a form in the human-made world. Nature-made and human-made: very similar. And to talk with me throughout the day would be helpful for on-the-spot interaction. Because you have free will, we need you to ask."

My Body Elemental as a Teacher

Sometimes when I arrived at the Amphitheater, Mano had beings with him whom he wanted me to meet. Once he came with a fairy on his shoulder, and as I moved closer she slipped off onto my shoulder. This happened a few times, and then she entered my body. I now know this being as Mara, my body elemental.

Our bodies are composed of the four physical elements of earth, air, fire, and water—and Mara communicates with me about the health and wellbeing of these parts. She lives, however, in the etheric, nonphysical level, and when I feel her presence it's in the etheric. I believe everyone has a body elemental, waiting to initiate this kind of dialogue; we are never alone. In addition to the presence of our guardian angel, who is always watching over us, our body elemental lives within us and is known as the body intelligence. I think of my body elemental as "she"; in truth it is both he and she, a spiritual being made up of the consciousness in all the elements of my body. She is of the spiritual dimension, wisely guiding the balance of all of my physical systems. Her goal is to keep my body alive and functioning with the perfection of my God nature. My friend Patricia practices this balancing work on her own body by noticing cells (which she sees as orbs) that are single colored, then visualizes their movement to higher full-spectrum rainbow orbs.

Mara is ever present and gives me impressions of what is needed to maintain my health and vitality. Once when I was recovering from an illness, she guided me to use a pendulum to discern which foods would support my recovery and which would hinder it. When I have the feeling of thirst, she is telling me that my body needs more water to function properly. When I feel full yet continue eating, she has to find a way to regain balance. A feeling of being bloated or releasing gas tells me that she's working to bring my body back into balance. She may also be saying, "Barbara, please don't do that again." I have seen two very large people fill their plates with lots of food and eat it all, then fill them a second time. My body elemental won't let me do that. She is quite insistent that if I eat beyond being full she will signal me with nausea. I used to ignore her warning and eat more food than my body wanted. Then I would throw up.

It is easy for me to fall into unconscious habits and act out emotional needs with body habits such as breathing shallowly or avoiding exercise. The point is to create a loving relationship with my body elemental so that I stay mindful and respect her needs. She creates my health, vitality, youth, and vigor, and I do not want to be at war and in competition with her. We have the same goals for me: to be happy and healthy, with the energy to live life fully, truly, and creatively.

I am developing the habit of speaking to Mara when I enter the bathroom. I think of this as her temple. Mara loves to hear me say "I love you" and "thank you". She appreciates my telling her what is going to happen, such as, "I have a five-hour drive ahead of me, I want you to be strong and energized when I get home." She likes things that are natural—the feel of organic cotton, silk, and wool clothing, the taste of fresh rather than canned vegetables, a small piece of good dark chocolate to bring balance at the end of a meal. She wants me to use natural remedies for normal care of my/her body: witch hazel for body pain and bruises, grapefruit seed extract for cold symptoms, a 15-minute horizontal rest daily when I feel fatigue.

Workers or Companions: The Little Ones

Once during my early days on the Mountain, I was double-digging an asparagus bed in my garden. On the third day, after digging a while, I sat back and sighed. With my inner eye, I saw a small gnome about one foot tall standing in front of me with his hands on his hips. He looked me in the eye and chided, "You haven't once asked for help." From that time on I have asked for help in all sorts of situations, particularly as I walk the stairs out of the Amphitheater. I began seeing funny images, like a gnome at the top of the stairs tossing a rope down to another gnome, who attached it to my belt. The one at the top pulled and the one behind me pushed to get me up the stairs. Sometimes I saw them on each side of me, holding my arms to help me up the stairs. I have named these two helpers Yo Ho and Heave Ho and have come to know them well, as representatives of the working, or companion, gnomes whom I call the "little ones."

Since I am a safe human and my soul has said yes, the little ones live with me and are usually present when I look with my inner, or etheric vision; I have learned to feel them first, and then I look to see what is happening. Sometimes I call them companions, helpers, or workers. They like being called workers, as they feel it gives them more stature for this project of building relationships with humans. My understanding is that they are learning and evolving through this service.

The workers offer help and protection and have been assigned to work with me in my home and with my activities, to make my life easier and safer however they can. They have suggested, for example, that I call on them and on the air elementals for strength every time I walk up stairs, pick up a heavy suitcase, or just need extra strength. To do this, I open my heart and ask for help on the in-breath, then move on the out-breath. This has given me great strength. I no longer need to hang onto the banister or huff and puff as I climb stairs. Some workers seem to

Yo Ho & Heave Ho

have specific skills, like the one who helps me with computer accuracy (when I remember to ask). They are delightful companions who love working with me and appreciate my asking them for help. They also love receiving appreciation for their assistance.

Another way the workers help, Mano has told me, is by giving me amusing pictures to grab my attention and keep my mind focused. When I detect them gamboling around, I'm reminded to expand my awareness and see if I can feel the presence of any "larger ones" around. "When you get into the habit of doing this regularly," Mano says, "you will build your own inner knowing and personal self."

When, years ago, Mano first brought a number of small elemental beings to live in my house and learn what a human is like, I thought I was making up this whole idea. My sensitivity gradually increased so that I could look within and picture what they were doing. Some of the pictures were so funny I had to believe they were real. I have learned that they are willing to be amusing, childlike, even foolish, to get my attention and to let me know they are outside my imagination. They are also so thoroughly in their own reality that they must stretch to make sense of the human foibles that arise from having freedom.

Once after I had washed my hair and was using the hair dryer, I felt activity around me and looked to see what was happening. Each elemental had a hair dryer and was blowing over its own head and then blowing the hot air at one another like children. Another time I was washing dishes and saw each of them with an apron on like mine, drying dishes. On my way to the hot tub one day I "saw" them in little old-fashioned one-piece striped bathing suits carrying beach balls, colorful inner tubes, and water wings. We all got into the hot tub, and while I soaked they played.

Another time, when I arrived in the Amphitheater, I felt the presence of a large group of little spirits around two feet tall. Although I had been aware of them before, this time they came close, formed a parade, and circled around me as I sat in the chair with the computer on my lap. When I asked, "Who are these little ones?" I got the answer, "They are the keepers of the land." I asked Mano, "Do they have any name I would know? I don't recognize them." He replied, "They are gnomes, but they look like themselves, not necessarily like pictures in a storybook. When there is a party or people come wanting to see gnomes, they put on their colorful clothes with the red pointed caps so they will be recognized. You are seeing them in their everyday work clothes of muted tones, similar to the earth colors you see in the Amphitheater. Have you noticed they feel much like the workers who live in your house?"

Traveling with the Little Ones

On my trip to Ireland the summer after Jim died in February 2004, Mano asked me to take some little ones with me, so they could visit their homeland. I agreed, with the thought that traveling with gnomes would add to the adventure. After saying *yes*, I didn't think much about these little ones until I was walking to the airplane, pulling my suitcase. I was aware of something going on behind me, and turning to look, saw with my inner sight five little gnomes, each pulling a small suitcase. As I settled in the plane, put my suitcase under the seat, and fastened my seat belt, I was again aware of them "fussing around," trying to hook their seatbelts. The engine of the plane started, and all hell broke loose. Suddenly I had five little gnomes shaking and quivering with fear on my lap. They were terrified with the noise and vibration of the airplane. I just held them and, once again, felt their reality.

On a free day in Ireland when I chose to stay in the manor house to catch up with myself, rest, and read, I again became aware of the little ones. They wanted me to come outside with them to the back garden. They had met some small local gnomes who didn't believe they were actually traveling with a human and wanted to see me, to have proof. My guys were bragging about traveling with "their human." I sat in the garden for a while and felt activity around me, though I didn't see or hear anything. Then I said goodbye and returned to my room. I felt my friends' gratitude and pride. For the remainder of the trip I was so busy with my own travels that I have little memory of them.

The Little Ones as Protectors

I realized the true value of the companions' protection when we had an enormous windstorm some years ago. The electricity went out, and limbs and branches were falling from the five large redwood trees in my yard. I had the opportunity to leave the Mountain and go to the beach to stay. When I returned, I was shocked to see limbs and branches piled four feet high in my front yard, making a solid covering approximately ten foot square. However, not one branch had landed on my house. Three young madrone trees did fall on the back of the house. They were tall and slim, approximately eight inches in diameter, piled neatly one on top of the other on the strongest part of the room structure. No window was broken, and the roof had no damage. The TV antenna was the only thing damaged, which was no problem since I don't watch TV. I was stunned with my good fortune, and deeply grateful. I had no doubt that the elementals had protected my home. I have six buildings on this three-acre piece of land. The only damage came from the top of a mature redwood tree that twisted off and pierced the kitchen roof of the guest cottage. In addition to the elementals' help, the men in my family came up and worked for days, cutting the limbs from the yard to be burned in the fireplace and chipping the branches to cover paths and the parking lot to the Amphitheater.

Elementals Protect the House in a Storm

The Council of Gnomes

PART THREE

WORKING WITH THE COUNCIL OF GNOMES, A PORTAL OF AWARENESS

2001–2017

COUNCIL FORMATION & PROCESS

AFTER MANO ASKED ME TO BEGIN meeting with the Council of Gnomes and writing down the proceedings on my computer in 2001, I established the habit of calling Council each week when I worked in the studio. Sometimes Mano would request additional meetings as well. I would sit on my chair, formally open the Council, then close my eyes and look within to see who was present. When I first started doing this I would see a circle of chairs with a speaker's table across from me. On each side of the room were bleachers where different beings watched the Council in operation. I sat within the circle, computer in my lap, and recorded the whole interaction as it happened.

"To begin," Mano told me, "we pass the love around, sending love into the center of the circle and letting it fill the space until each of us is surrounded by the love of all of us pooled together. This way we share and build the power. Each one of us receives more love than we give, because it multiplies geometrically. Then we can communicate from within this shared space of equality and heart love. Remember, energy is spirit—and, I would add, spirit is love. So this is the shared love space that we bring back to our own energy field. You will notice we each contribute a different color, and you add a white light—the Christ light we all need for our new stage of evolution. Together we create a sparkly crystal rainbow light."

The studio feels like a sanctuary, a holy space, with its high ceiling and a glass wall at one end looking out into the trees. It's a good Council space and, through years of regularly meeting there, my relationship with the gnomes has grown strong and trustworthy. We continually fine-tune the process, and the configuration of the gathering changes according to the need. The only consistent aspect, I say, is that it's always changing. In the first year or two, the goal was to move me into heart relating. "Be in your heart," they continually reminded me. "Look and see where your energy is; learn to check it often."

Now, when I'm in a period of going to the studio regularly (sometimes another project will keep me away for a while), I do an overnight retreat. As soon as I arrive, usually in the afternoon, I open Council and check on what we want to work on or accomplish. Then I spend much of the night journaling and connecting, using my laptop. I usually do art the next day, or perhaps I will start a painting after the Council meeting so that I can wake up in the morning and see a new aspect of the work-in-progress. It's a back-and-forth process: paint, then move away to capture the image through different eyes.

Elementals come to Council to learn, to receive training for working with humans, even to be corrected on errant behavior.

(Once I glimpsed an observation room that was glassed off so that ignorant, discordant energies could learn by watching the Light at work.) The one who sits at the speaker's table changes. "We change roles so that you can begin to recognize us from our energy," Mano once said, "and not just automatically call the one in the speaking chair by the name you have learned in the past. Soon you will be able to see what we wear. Each one who comes represents a different order of Faerie; we are a Council

Mano

of different groups coming together. We meet ahead of time to prepare our talks with you. We are adjusting our ranks to find the combination that works best.

Many are participating in this project, watching from something similar to remote viewing on a TV screen. They watch our energy exchange as well as our conversation."

"Notice how ideas come," Mano told me. "You write them down, then together we build and refine them beyond your ability to receive. We both learn in the process. It is not that we in the gnome realm have this all together and are feeding it to you little by little. We have the concept and know where we are going, but we need your input to express it in words that make sense to you, and then to your friends."

Another time I was told: "Simply keep focused on your priority, your commitment, your desire to serve the Mother. Maturity is a great consideration. You have noticed the stature of the gnomes who came when the Council was first called. They were and are mature gnomes within their field of connection and service. Those of us you are working with now are not of their stature. The ones who came first were like master beings within the gnome world. We are mature and in service to the masters, doing their work, under their guidance. We are the teachers. The masters stay attuned to the connection between you and your teachers. There is no need for them to hang around when you are not consistently present or ready to become a mature member of this work, this team, this Council. The companions, or as you call them, 'the little ones,' are always with you. They are in training and one day will be teachers."

TRANSITION AFTER JIM'S DEATH

IN THE SUMMER OF 2003, JIM AND I HAD GREAT FUN planning a trip to live in Europe the next summer. We were going to join Mara Freeman on a tour of sacred sites in Ireland and end the trip on a tour of sacred sites with R.J. Stewart, our teacher of the Faerie faith, in England and Wales. In February 2004, Jim died. I felt the call to travel as we had planned, but I was clear I didn't want to live in Europe that summer without Jim. I finally decided to take a friend with me on the Ireland trip, and then another friend to England and Wales.

The night that Jim died, I stayed with him for a while. When I went back to bed, I heard an audible voice say, "Will the real Barbara Thomas please step forward?" I was shocked, and then I realized that in all my 77 years I had never lived alone. I wondered who the real Barbara Thomas was. At that moment I felt the call to adventure and to discovery. Now, with Jim's passing and my children out of the home, I was freed from the day-to-day roles and responsibilities of wife and mother and could give my time and attention to the journaling, conversations, and guidance that would move me into the larger part of myself.

A week after Jim's death I recorded the following. "You were wise to come to Council," the gnomes told me. "The tides of emotion could sweep you away. There is much to be done, as you take over the home and business to guide for yourself. As for your health and daily activities, we ask you to stay connected with us. It is vitally important, and we stand ready to be of assistance to you. As we have said before, it is for our evolution as well as yours."

A few weeks later, in Council, a large gnome stood across from me with three others on each side. The small ones were standing and sitting on the floor in front of the larger ones. "I come with appreciation for this latest call to service," I said. "I appreciate working with the small ones."

"Take a gnome representative with you to Ireland," I heard in response, "to keep yourself connected with our reality. Your trip to Ireland, the homeland, is very important, particularly at this time when the stars are opening gates for you to walk through, as your original self, toward your true service. You must be open and present. We propose sending along a group of workers to be present within your aura, to stay closely connected with you and your work. They, in turn, will be able to learn from the homeland, to reconnect with their ancestors and their own ancestral memory. Your wake-up process and the work you are calling the 'real Barbara Thomas stepping forth' is in place. All you need to do is move step by step. We too will be with you as you travel. Enjoy the beauty, the people, your companions. You will be leaving the old and entering the new as you walk through the airport in Los Angeles.

"Your heart is healing well," the Council communication continued. "You yourself are surprised at how well your grieving process is going. You are receiving much help from us and from your other spirit friends. We have no intention of losing the momentum that has been set in place. Jim's leaving was in divine order and divine timing. The dark of the moon at Jim's death and birth were your clues to the appropriateness of it all. Stay attentive to the moment and what needs to be done in the present. Each moment will lead to the next, throughout your life. To jump ahead and question what being alone will be like in a year or two is totally inappropriate and even harmful. Last night was the first time you've done that, as you were thinking of your friends Millie and Rosemary and wondering how they're feeling now that their partners have died. They are not you. You have work to do on many levels, and you have help on many levels. Stay present with your breath and with the inner vision of your team and yourself."

Mano then said, "I would speak. I urge you to slow down as you transcribe our words. Have no self-consciousness. It is my responsibility to speak, and it is yours to write, removing your mind from the process. I will be your major guide through Ireland. Mara, your body elemental, will be ever present with me. You will learn a great deal, as we have set this up as a learning and a remembering time—a reconnection. You can look to us as your constant companions. The workers will be there also; when you look for us, then look for them. We are your teachers and wayfinders; the workers will make life easier and amusing as you connect with them. Thank you for answering the call. I will guide you in many ways to co-create with us. We are all pleased with this stage of your work. Do not speak to anyone about it, because it is too new; wait to speak until the work is well established."

The major purpose of my first trip to Ireland turned out to be about connecting with the Neolithic within myself. I had very few conscious times of communicating with the little ones who were accompanying me, though I did experience hearing their voices when they asked me to come out and meet the local elementals. Now, looking back, I realize that they were with me, looking after me, throughout the trip. At Loughcrew, for example, the familiarity of my hand touching the carvings on the entrance stone brought tears. I lay for a while inside the cairn, realizing that I had been there before and was returning home. Knowing that other people were waiting to come in, I got up and came out. I lay on the wet grass with light drizzle falling on me, still crying. As I look inside myself now, years later, I see the little ones there with me, surrounding me in the cairn and on the grass, comforting me and acknowledging my return to source. When I sat up on the grass, my heart was touched as I saw a double rainbow stretched from horizon to horizon, all across Ireland. I recognized this as a "sign along the highway".

Staying in Health and Equilibrium

In a Council meeting several months later, after I returned from Europe, I told the five gnomes sitting in front of me, "I am so sorry I have been careless with this amazing connection. I am afraid I have only thought of it from my own perspective of spiritual contact. I have not thought of it as a commitment to keep connected or with the realization that you are depending on me. I have been very careless and self-centered; I deeply apologize. In addition, or as a result, my body has gotten out of balance with jet lag and pushing myself."

The gnomes responded: "We have watched you go through indifference and then turmoil over getting settled after Jim's death. We wonder why you have not remembered the stability you receive by connecting with our dimension of life and our Council. It has been necessary for us to allow your body to get out of balance since you did not volunteer to come to us. We didn't cause the imbalance, just allowed it. Your health and wellbeing for the past few years have been to a certain extent due to our care of your body, which is the vehicle we are using to make inroads into the consciousness of humanity. In one sense you are experiencing what we see over and over with humans. You lose consciousness of the reality of our connection. It becomes a lark or hobby. We want you to reconsider what we actually are doing here and look again at your part and your commitment. We are building a bridge between nature and human. We are focusing on the evolution of the planet by calling our human counterpart to task and to consciousness. Our need is to speak with humans so that the words we speak will flow into humanity's consciousness and thus into the human mental field. You are our broadcast station and we are the broadcasters. At some time this may go the other way, when you are more aware and have more knowledge of the needs of people or the needs of earth, as you see it from your human perspective."

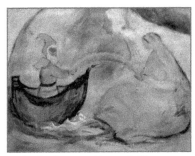

Bridge Between Nature & Human

My body elemental, Mara, then spoke of how I could regain a healthy balance. "Open your heart to receive," she counseled. "Feel the pressure and power entering from the earth, through your feet into your heart. As you develop the habit of holding your awareness centered in your heart, you will find yourself feeling more nourished and more attuned to the plants and people around you. The only way you can hear Spirit is through your heart. You will notice that as you feel your heart energy your feet get tingly, for you have also aligned with your root and earth chakras. Your efforts to build your energy level are a blessing for us and for all who touch your aura. You have already been given the way to do this. Touch your heart at the center of the breastbone, drop your energy, your consciousness into the center of the earth, pull the earth energy back up to your heart, and then move that earth power to do what needs to be done."

The Council continued: "When you experience chest pain, as you did recently, do not think you are ill or in danger. As long as you stay conscious and in communication we will be able to move your body through the changes necessary. You will not need to get sick to make the changes. That is totally not in order."

During this type of "elemental body work" I was told to lie on the earth. They were "rewiring" me, the elementals said, reconnecting me to parts of myself that had been severed long ago. They didn't tell me what these parts were, as they wanted me to experience the healing on my own and know it was truly happening. If they had been specific, they speculated, I might have thought I was creating from their suggestions. Another similar experience came when I was lying on the ground between two mature madrone trees. My inner listening heard a voice in my head saying, "We need to attune and adjust your body." I saw small elementals, one-half inch in height, moving all over my body, aligning my energies with spirit, raising my vibration into the frequency of my higher chakras. Adjusting my emotions and physical body are a constant working needed to bring my human consciousness into a more harmonious frequency with nature. Then I can truly be of service.

I remember that the first time I saw the elementals working on my body was in 1967, when my friend Brooks had brought me a manuscript to read, one inspired by her elemental companion oh den du. I had been sick in bed for several days, and as I opened the envelope I saw inch-high gnomes tumble out. They moved quickly over my body, digging and planting seeds that looked like

peas. Every so often they would pull out a dry, withered seed and replace it with a fresh one. It was all over in less than a minute. This made an enormous impact on me, as at the time I was not really sure I believed in elementals.

During one Council meeting, I worked with my inner self, BarBara, on healing prolapsed muscles. "To start the twelve weeks of I AM statements is the next focus of integration and will bring forth great fruit," she counseled. "I realize you are just completing twelve weeks of focus on the prolapsed muscles within your body, and

BarBara

so far you are not seeing any significant change. You have more to learn in the field of visualization and feeling. At the same time, I encourage you to acknowledge what you have accomplished. Hold the feeling-vision for those muscles to return to their vibrant youth and intensify that picture to support the general 'youthing' of all cells within your body.

'Youthing' means full rainbow cells with no depletion of color. The violet ray is helpful in this work, as it consumes any sludge that has covered the colors within the cells or drained their life force. Life force is the full rainbow, so again, wrap your body in a rainbow and each cell will pull in what it needs as that sludge of doubt, judgment, and negative thinking is removed. Joy is in the fullness of life and this is what is waiting as we integrate with Starlight."

Starlight Speaks

The Moon Ritual

Shortly after Jim's death I created an altar on a small table in the center of the house where I would pass it whenever I moved around. I lit a candle each morning and let it burn all day in front of the Black Madonna, whom I have named Mother Earth. This ritual became a member of my family and blessed me each time I walked past Mother Earth and saw the candle. It filled some of the vacant space in my heart as I adjusted to my new life.

The idea for the ritual came after I fell in love with a picture of Myra Twery, an Indian woman. I looked up her story and then bought her book. She works with Divine Mother in all ways, and though I didn't take up Indian cooking to the extent she taught, I felt compelled to do the moon ritual that she did with her family all of her life. I did this for three years, and it enabled me to open to Starlight—my God Self, true self, higher consciousness—and let her write to me and guide me.

Ascended Master Teachings

Another gift that came after Jim died was a magical happening that the Council created to guide me to connect with the Radiant Rose Academy. They directed me to an online spiritual curriculum of Ascended Master Teachings. These teachings have given me concepts and names for energies I've felt and experiences I've had but did not know how to articulate or even understand. I have found my spiritual home with this organization and am ever grateful to Mother Akasha for her gentle, loving, deep, and profound teachings.

The Ascended Master path follows the Christ path, carrying the energy of father/mother God, light/love, heart/mind and embodying the God within. It works with the sacred fire, which holds the colors of the rainbow. In the fall from grace, we separated ourselves from God and from the divine feminine; now the call is to reactivate the interaction between our own higher self and our ascended and angelic family, rediscovering our individual divine plan.

A few of the teachings that help inform my core Ascended Master practices have to do with the four elements, earth, water, air, and fire.

- *Earth* (related to the goddess Virgo): I walk on the earth to be energized and revivified–to receive the life-giving essence of the electronic force and the magnetic currents within the earth. With my every step on the earth I am receiving energy, vitality, life, and substance from Mother Earth herself.

- *Water* (related to the god Neptune): Each time I take a drink of the water element I receive the electronic force of Father Neptune's own heart. This water element pours through my bloodstream, carrying liquid light that becomes purified life-giving energy and substance for my physical form; I cannot be depleted.

- *Air* (related to the god Ares): With every breath I am receiving the electronic force of light substance in the air element (Father Ares). I am constantly energizing myself. Nothing can ever oppose me, and nothing can disturb me because I am accepting the fullness of God's presence, God's energy, and God's substance in and as myself.

- *Fire* (related to the god Helios): The Sun (Father Helios) constantly pours forth the electronic force of cosmic light rays to this entire system of worlds. I acknowledge this, accept it, and feel it floating and penetrating the flesh of my atomic body. From the shift of December 22, 2012, when we moved into the Golden Age, Father Helios is consistently raising the vibrational frequency being sent to earth to

Elementals Bless the Land

lift humanity to a higher consciousness level, from the third to the fifth dimension.

At one Council, after I had connected with the Ascended Master Teachings, the beings present expressed enthusiasm for my work. "You have been consciously connecting with what you call your angel team to help and to work with you on your projects. We wholeheartedly endorse this development, which was your idea, not ours. What we see happening for you is a stronger connection with both the angelic and Faerie worlds. This makes the cord of relationship stronger and more varied. Soon you will truly be living in two worlds, a state that was prophesied so many years ago when you lived in La Cañada. The direction is always for you to choose, and you seem to be choosing this double reality more and more. It can be a rich creative life. What it brings to our side of the veil is more and varied spirit beings who are available to interact with humans. This enlivens their own service to the One as well as increasing the strands of consciousness by intimately looking into a human mind, sensing and feeling the harmony between body, mind, and spirit."

Rama Leaves, Ramala Arrives

Rama, my angel teacher, temporarily left after Jim died. As an overseer of the project, he was off learning how to relate with this next phase of our work, and Ramala came in his place. She was more a teacher than Rama and was probably the one who guided me to Myra Twery and her book containing the moon

Ramala

ritual. I often attuned to Ramala during Council, and in one 2005 meeting she explained: "Barbara is your outer mind, the surface self; BarBara is the inner mind, the inner being; Starlight is the I AM presence, the God within." Before I was able to interact with nature beings through my inner vision and hearing, I would see little squiggles of light zipping past my face, or points of light flashing on and off in front of me. One of the first inner visions I saw was a light like a star in the sky. It impacted me as a presence, and years later I met Starlight, my higher self. These three—Barbara, BarBara, and Starlight—along with Mano, became my major teachers during this time. I have recently received an elaboration on the different parts of myself and their unique means of expression. "Barbara" is described as the mental, intellectual, closed-mind part of myself that I was born with, the unawakened self. I learned that in the Aramaic language, "Bar" means "child of" and "Bara" means "nature." "BarBara" is the child-of-nature part that interacts with angels and has opened to creative expression, the imaginative, the artist.

One day, after some disturbing journaling about being afraid of success and a Tarot reading in which Death was the signature card, I came to my studio and saw that the Council had already formed. Gnomes were on the side and a female figure was across from me. After the greetings, I asked about this feminine being and she replied: "I am BarBara, the honored guest, the earth light, the faerie queen, the original self. So many names have been used to name my consciousness. All work and all are true; all are called upon to keep your outer mind active and involved in the process. 'Entertained' is another word to express what we have had to do with your mind, Barbara. Do you truly understand how important your outer mind is, your Barbara mind? You are the guard, you are the awareness of what may enter and what needs to be kept out and transformed to be of value for our work.

"I have not appeared to you in this way before, though the work you do with this Council and in your studio is part of my work within your life and within the world—my work through you. Your pondering about whether you are afraid, willing, or allowing success is so vitally important that I want to be a part of this consciously with you. It is true that you have allowed success, and it has come in many ways and forms. You have not felt worthy because you knew you only *allowed* it but were not instrumental in *creating* it. There have been exceptions, like the CFO training manual, when you were able to create successfully for others. Now it is time to shift and create success with your own work, for your true Self. This is so intertwined with the collective and old consciousness of limitation, fear of success, fear of power, fear of being controlled. It is all your old stuff, Barbara.

Child of Nature

"The new is to open to Spirit, to do the work in and through your spiritual guidance. You are also to show others how this can be done—to awaken their memory banks and activate strands of DNA that have been dormant. You still harbor the erroneous concept of the Old Age that success has to do with money, business, and public acclaim—all outer show. True success is to express yourself wholeheartedly, giving your full attention to the goal and allowing the inspired ideas to come from within. You are to take each step with heartful ease and openness.

"In many lifetimes, your personalities accepted the idea of failure because of what outside people expected. Yet from inside, from the exact work that wanted to be done, the work was highly successful. You died thinking yourself a failure, and this is being cleared now. At your birthday the transition period will be complete and the new opened. The part of you that we relate with is deeper than your daily outer life. We deal with the eternal Starlight self, not Barbara, although you, Barbara, are the one who needs to come forth. It is all unfolding and will become clearer for you as we continue."

Once in the meditation room at CFO, I was lying on the floor in front of the altar. Later a friend who was there with me told me of her vision. She saw me as a nun who had just died and was placed in front of the altar. The nun's spirit stepped out of her body, looked at it, and passed judgment: "Too easy, not enough joy; seven lives was too long to remain in the church."

After the burning times, I realized I could no longer serve Mother Nature by living in the forest but could only serve her by joining the church. I had a vision of being a nun in a lifetime when I entered the church as a young gypsy girl who had fallen in love with Jesus. She wanted to live in the big monastery on the hill in a safe, settled environment—no more traveling and living at the edge of society. She wanted to live where she could worship Jesus in the beautiful church with its incense and candles. In this vision I saw the young girl running away from the gypsy camp with her heart wide open, her arms up over her head, running to join the church. In the next scene she ran into the stone wall protecting the property. It was not the dream she desired. The church authorities used her psychic abilities for their own education and information. She was disappointed, and her gypsy family would not take her back.

In a Council exchange the gnomes explained, "Your mind is the mind we work through, your vocabulary and understanding. Your lives spent in the church have placed a block of fear upon your natural knowing and abilities. Some of those early lives were still very much connected with nature, whereas many of the later ones were not—the ones that were too much for too long. Those lives embodied the fear. We have been guiding you gently to move away from that imposed fear, used to control you. The transition is nearly complete. Studying the Tarot and working with teachers who are bringing new points of view and new light will soften this resistance; working with those of the old, heavy way will impede your progress.

"The call to come home has gone out for all parts of your consciousness. Many parts of Self are preparing to return now that the I AM is clearly in place as the dominant structure within your personality. I smile at your surprise that this is so. It has been so easy and gentle; your willingness and my skill have caused this to go almost without notice, as a thief steals into the night–though in this case it is the honored guest arriving at the banquet. I smile at the simplicity of it all."

As the Council ended, I inquired about Mano. "I am here, Barbara," he assured me, "and have been honored and interested in this conversation." Then I asked about Ramala, and Mano said, "She is always present, even when she has no need to speak. Just know and appreciate her orchestration of these activities."

Lapses and Reminders: The Work

In the summer of 2005, I described going to a Council in which I felt as if a change was occurring that I didn't understand. "I don't know what is expected of me, or what the new plan is," I worried. "I may have been given teaching and I just don't remember. I have not printed out the teachings for a long time. I plan to do that job next week, when I take the week to honor the new moon. In the future I will print them out each week. Perhaps it would be better to do it each day, but that feels difficult. Last week I was asked to read at noon and I didn't remember–a result of the 'lost will' that the goddess-feeling side of life can heal."

In this same vein of humility and resolution, I spoke also of the difficulty I have in remembering to properly close sessions with the elementals and angels. "For you, the opening is easier to remember than the closing," the Council had told me. "This can be your point of awareness as you build the beauty path of healing and balance. Closing supports the wholeness that keeps your energies with you and not spread out among the teams you have called upon but are not currently working with. It would even be helpful to do a general closure periodically, in case you haven't remembered at the natural closing time." My plan for supporting this heightened consciousness was to do a 21-day program to establish the habit of conscious endings.

To support this, I decided to hold 20-second segments of time during the day to feel the joy and power of completions. This idea of dividing time into segments of intention is consistent with Rama's overarching teaching on how to live my day, and also coheres with Mano's statement, "Time is not governed by the hands of a clock but by segments of intention." The practice is to align with my God Self and with the workers, then say what I want to happen in that segment.

Mano, in another dialogue, spoke of the Council's purpose: "The wisdom and structure of earth is the focus of our service, to assist the evolution of the planet and encourage planetary beings to return in consciousness to God's openness and to

Planetary Logos

the planetary logos as a cell within the solar logos." I had the insight: "I see you are having me focus on gnome consciousness to keep me grounded in my body, to bring spirit to matter rather than my attempting to leave my body in order to be spiritual. I am to be spiritual *in* the body; this will feed the cells of my body, the cells of the earth, the consciousness of gnome and earth beings."

"You have it right, Barbara," Mano replied. "We often need to rephrase something to you many times. One reason our teachings sometimes appear contradictory is that we look for words that make sense to you. We think we have it and then see by your actions and thoughts that it is not quite right. You step into choices in areas you know little about, and drag on actions where you know you are the only one who can make the choice." In reply I lamented, "So often when I hear the information you have just given me I feel that it is nothing new, that I have heard it before. I wonder if I am just saying the same things to myself over and over." Mano understood my dilemma: "In one way that is true. It is the same information over and over. The difference is that I AM SPEAKING TO YOU. You are not speaking to yourself. Until you move into the naturalness of the process, remembering easily with confidence, I will continue to say the same thing. It is imperative for this basic information to become second nature to you. It will come. We do not want you to get sick in order to work these things through; we want you to do it with ease, accepting the love and grace that is always available. You are never alone. You are never to work alone. Always consult with the wise ones of the earth before you do a major activity. They can see the larger picture and the flow of energies."

"I feel the desire for you to teach me the ways of the earth," I said in Council. "I read what has been taught to others and try to learn and understand. Will you ever be my teacher in this way?" The reply was: "We already are, Barbara. It is subtle. You have not recognized much that we teach. You have not remembered much. As you get back into the teachings and make them part of your life and consciousness, more will be given. We are not holding back from you. We are carefully monitoring your capacity. Ramala has been guiding this process, for she is your teacher." Ramala adds, "As the little gnomes are not

Gifts and Promises

yet able to converse with you, so on some levels you are not yet able to converse with us. This is all natural, as we have been teacher and student for many lives. BarBara knows me well, and I have been with you, Barbara, from the beginning, to be able to accomplish exactly what we are doing at this time. You will know me better as time goes on."

The Appendix contains two of my transcripts of Council meetings and both of them feature my ongoing, striving process of coming into alignment with my destiny path, the lapses that pull me out of that alignment, and the reminders from my

Council to realign. The gnomes' understanding and patience with this process has been remarkable, and my dedication to it, even through the lapses, has been the center of my life and also strikes me as remarkable.

THE COUNCIL ASKS FOR HELP

"IT IS A HARD TIME ON PLANET EARTH. There is much sadness and fear. We are called upon in many and varied ways to bring balance to the internal structure of the planet, to hold her on a balanced course. The emotional bodies of many throughout humanity are so out of balance they are causing a dangerous situation for the Mother. We need humans with heart to counterbalance the mistakes that are being contemplated. Work with us to keep your own life in equilibrium and harmony, stay rested and keep your vibrations high, so that you can be part of the solution and not add to the problem. We can no longer go on alone. We are in deep need of the feeding we receive from interacting with the human kingdom, and you are in deep need of us to sustain your life by interacting with nature. Our simplest request is that you recognize the life force within soil, air, and water, and acknowledge the green and growing things as living beings. Speak to us, relate, and if you have use of our bodies, give thanks for that gift."

I remind myself that this is a planet of evolution, change, and choice. The spirits of the land are being awakened. My participation in this awakening is part of my soul path and service to the earth. I do this by relating and showing respect, expressing love and appreciation, speaking to the plants, touching them with love, speaking to the faces I see in the trees, hills, and on the ground. I ask questions of nature through a tree or animal, then listen for answers.

Singing and dancing on the earth creates a vibration and serves as a wake-up call to the elementals. I have been told that the monthly circle dance Jim and I held in the Amphitheater for many years, and that I still do three times a year, was received as a blessing to the land and the trees. When I attended a Native

American celebration with drumming and the simple Ghost Step Dance, I saw it as a true blessing for the nature beings because of the very intentionality and consciousness of the dancers.

Once, as I walked to the Amphitheater, I began singing a prayer song. My vision shifted and I saw a man's face in the leaves on the path. I sat down and made a drawing of the face. He then spoke to me and said that he was called forth by my song. "Be aware," he said, "that when you lift your vibration you are also lifting the vibration of the planet. The substance of our bodies is made up of the four elements of earth, water, air, and fire, as is the substance of our planet. At this time it is imperative for you to focus on having a grounded, expanded heart. We need this to be an established fact for you from this time forth. We work in joy as we work with you. This joy comes from our grateful hearts. We invite you to open your own grateful heart as you walk on earth or work in the garden. This nurtures and blesses us and we are deeply grateful."

I have heard that the earth frequency is very deep and slow, whereas the frequency of electricity is very high and fast. Humanity today is seldom out of the range of electrical influence, which causes our minds to race and everything to speed up. I am often asked to lie on the earth so that the nature spirits can have clear access to the cellular structure of my body for adjustments and attunements, to get me back in balance and harmony with earth's vibration. They say, "This makes it easier for us to relate with you." When I was first awakening, I read that the new Hubble telescope shows the universe expanding. My inner knowing (input from my Council) said to me that God is ever expanding, which means that there is no goal, no end to be reached, only and always expansion to be more than I was before. My divine plan has to do with being of service to Mother Earth.

"As you walk on the earth, ask to be shown how to interact with each particular place. For you to practice connecting with the beings of the land, hearing and speaking to them is the important thing at this point. This develops your skill and increases your experience and confidence. It also awakens and encourages the nature beings of each location. We need to speak with humans. We want our words to flow into the human mental field so that those who do not speak to us directly can receive our teachings and requests telepathically. The simple opening is Hello Mother, then hello to the angel of the place and the elementals of the land. Once you establish a deep connection with a particular place in nature, those nature beings need your presence to stay connected with the human world. When you are not there and do not think of them, they fade back into their own inner world, which does not include humans."

I've had two friends tell me that in the Amphitheater they saw something like spiderwebs going in all directions, carrying rainbow light out to the world and to human consciousness. Periodically the gnomes have referred to this, saying that the angels track the energies of everyone who has ever come to the Amphitheater in order to nourish and support humans so they will awaken. It is done through this web, like dew on a spider web, like droplets of rainbow colors.

The Council has asked me to hold a holy space for them in my heart, to pray for the protection of the elements and for the cleansing of air, water, and earth. "Elementals have served and protected you throughout time; now you can do the same for them. Each prayer starts a huge movement within consciousness. This is why the Great Master asked you to pray without ceasing. Your prayers give permission for the cosmic intelligences that guard and guide the planet to more easily influence and inspire people in positions of power to make wise choices regarding nature. To hold your energy in your heart is prayer. To be peaceful, tranquil, and joyful is prayer. To set intentions for the things you want to happen is prayer. We call you and all humanity home to the house of prayer and world service. Amen."

Gifts and Promises

One of the advantages to living a long life is that I can look back and see in things being revealed today the seeds that actually were planted 20, 30, and even 40 years ago. I am grateful to know that

I have been guided so carefully and lovingly. I am not alone. My Council goes before me and prepares the way. I live in gratitude.

On the morning of my 88th birthday I received a gift, an experience, an intervention and a teaching.

I went to the Amphitheater early in the morning to greet the beings of the land and lie down to feel the earth enter my body. Soon I became aware of a line of spirit beings walking in a circle around me. They walked a figure 8 around my body, continuing to make a second figure 8, using the bottom circle of the first eight as the top of the second. They walked this path a couple of times. Next they pulled the third circle up to blend with the second circle, then pulled the second to blend with the first. At this point I became aware of a teaching: They started with two 8s, naming my 88th birthday and then pulled the circles up until I had one circle, a zero, or nothing. At this point they informed me: "From now on you are not to think of age. People have fixed ideas of what an elder is capable of. We do not want their limiting thought forms to interfere with the process we are working within you."

The Ascended Master Teachings say that as we move into the Seventh Golden Age the dispensation for dying has been removed, though some may choose to stay and be of service. I consider this to be out of my hands. I have made two promises to God. The first was when we were living in the Los Angeles area and people were prophesying that Los Angeles would slide into the ocean. To stay out of fear, I made a promise: "In a body or out of a body, I serve God." Once I got my priorities straight, I prayed in peace. The prophecy timing passed and Los Angeles stayed in place. Human nature is so delightfully amusing. One woman who was part of my prayer group was angry that the prophecy wasn't fulfilled, saying, "I prayed all night and nothing happened." I made the second promise after buying the Amphitheater, and it was instrumental in our moving to the Mountain the next year. Hanna, who owned the cottage that is now my home, sent me a music score written by her friend Don Howe while he was working in the Amphitheater. The title was, "Oh Lord, I will go where you want me to go and I will stay as long as you need me." Deep within my heart I knew this was also my truth.

Another gift that came along in this period of time took the form of the Garden Master Gnome. Andrea Boone has worked with me in the garden for many years. On one of these occasions I was sitting next to the lemon verbena tree with my back to the greenhouse, embraced by the tree's fragrance as we prepared for meditation with the garden angels and elementals. Andrea opened the seven directions, we chanted to still time, space, and motion, and then she invited the garden angel, the angel of Amity, and all the spirit beings associated with this land to join us.

Within my inner eye I saw an old gnome with a long beard standing about three feet high and looking at me directly in my face. He was different, not like the others I have seen working in the garden. His clothes were dark, his gray beard went almost to his knees, and I don't know if he had a hat or not. I simply observed him, face to face, without communicating, until Andrea guided the meditation to go into the deep earth to connect with the Goddess of the land. She asked the Goddess to

Spirits of the Land

bless the garden, the plants, and nature spirits. Immediately the gnome came back into my vision. He was excited to receive the blessing of the Goddess. I said to him, "I am surprised. I would think that she blesses you all of the time." Thoughts brought his words into my mind: "Yes, she does bless us all of the time and that is like everyday blessings. But when a human asks her to bless the garden and the nature spirits, it enhances her blessing a thousand-fold and it becomes a big celebration, like a birthday or Christmas." I realized that he looked similar to another gnome friend I relate with when I enter the Faerie sanctuary under the Amphitheater. I asked if his name was Lov-o-lay. He said, "No, but I am of the same stature as that one."

"I have had a garden in this part of the land for 25 years," I told him. He was well aware of that, he said, because he has been with me from the beginning. "I came," he said, "when you and Jim started your garden and made the big intention to have it be a healing spot on the planet, a homeopathic dose helping human and nature spirits work in conscious cooperation and harmony. Your prayer was that it would go out to heal the whole planet and open love, respect, and harmonious interaction between human beings and nature beings. That kind of an intention rang throughout the halls within the earth." He heard and answered the call because he wanted to work with us. He liked being with Jim when he would sit in the driveway and carefully pull the weeds from between the rocks. Jim never knew he was there, as I had not known of his presence before, but he likes working with us and with our land. He has taken it as his responsibility to keep the garden beautiful. Even though I do not work there as much as I used to, it still always looks good. This has surprised me and I call it a sweet garden. He is the one bringing the sweetness. Two years ago he brought the wild ferns into the north bed, which gives the garden a rich, vibrant energy all summer.

As I was ready to leave he told me he has shown himself to me as very old, with his long gray beard and subtle clothes, because he wanted me to recognize him as one of the old ones, the wise ones. He is part of the group I refer to as the Master Gnomes who live within the land. Now as I write this he stands in front of me, so I will become aware of another bit of information he wants me to recognize. My being able to see him, and his ability to communicate with me, is in response to a daily prayer I have been making for two or three weeks. Each day I go outside and speak to Mother Earth, telling her I know it is hard for her to make this shift upon her axis with ease and grace. I realize that if she didn't have to deal with humanity's fear and discordant energy it would be simple for her. Since that is not true, she shudders as she makes her shift, with a little earthquake here and a tornado there. I tell her I am sorry. I want to do my part to make it easier for her. I promise that I will shift within my own consciousness to support her as she makes her shifts. The Master Garden Gnome wants me to identify my ability to see and hear him so clearly as evidence of the subtle shift I am making and the answers I am receiving to my requests.

BREAKING THE LAW OF LOVE—& MY LEG

ENTERING AN ANCIENT NEOLITHIC SACRED SITE on my last trip to Ireland, my foot slipped on wet moss as I entered a sacred chamber going deep into the earth. My head gently rested on the entrance stone carved with symbols. I became aware of a flow of energy from the stone into my mind and of a message:"When you turn 80 (in three months) your life is going to change. You will start living the second book of your life. Not the second chapter. A whole new book."

Two months after I turned 80, my friend Andrea and I created a ritual of dedication to Mother Earth and the 12 acres of land on which I live. Our plan was to gift to the center of the land a ring that was meaningful to me and another ring to each of the four directions.

Eating breakfast the day before the dedication, I became aware of a spirit presence in the house. With my inner eye I was amazed to see beings sitting on every chair and couch in the three rooms I could see from the kitchen table—15 in all. I had never seen them before; actually, I had never seen anything like this before. I didn't know it at the time, but I now know they were the "spirits of the land", an aspect of my Council of Gnomes. They had come to bless me before I went on my dedication journey the next day.

The first stop on the journey was a small circle of five redwood trees in the center of the land. I made a prayer of dedication and gave my engagement ring to Mother Earth with the same commitment and dedication I gave to Jim and our marriage. Next we went up to Hill Top, in the direction of the west. As we walked through the forest I was telling Andrea an amusing story of an experience I'd had with a friend. Talking and not looking where I was walking, I stepped on something that twisted and I fell. As I fell, I had the thought *This is serious* and I heard a voice say, "This is a gift, Barbara." My leg was broken, my perineal nerve severed. Its healing took seven months in bed with many healers, massage therapists, electromagnetic therapy, prayer, essential oils–the whole works. At the end of this time, I was driving and walking with the energy reentering the nerve. My greatest joy was that I could once again sit cross-legged.

I had heard the inner voice many times before this. I know to trust it. I waited to discover what the gift might be. I was surprised and now acknowledge it as a precious gift–a hard way to learn, yet oh so valuable. As I lay in bed listening to Ascended Master Teachings, I learned of the five human habits: criticism, condemnation, judgment, blame, and gossip. When I was telling Andrea the "amusing" story, I realized I was indulging in four of the five habits. I now name these "Harmful Human Habits" and I link them in opposition to the Law of Love. This brought an amazing change in my life, since much of my previous conversation had involved criticism and judgment. These human habits were not only deeply engrained in my own mind and consciousness, but they also permeate the collective consciousness. I not only indulged them from within but also was bombarded from without.

By learning not to indulge in the harmful human habits I began to experience wonderful, creative, fun conversations with friends and strangers. I also completed two major projects: writing the book *Celebrating the Magic of Jim's Road* and writing the script for the DVD *Healing Burned Woman*. The Council of Gnomes blog also became a vital contribution to the service.

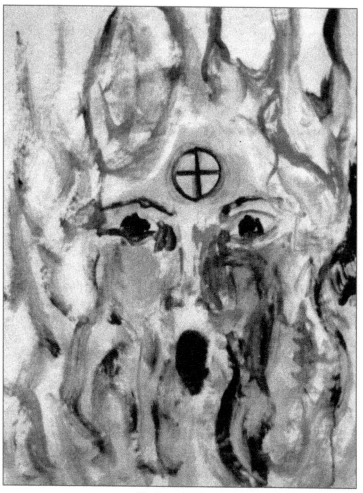

The Burned Woman

PART FOUR

BURNED WOMAN'S STORY

THE STORY ARRIVES

ABOUT FIVE YEARS AFTER MOVING TO THE MOUNTAIN, I had an unusual experience. While talking to Olivia on the phone, my inner sight opened and I saw a woman with dark skin walking toward me. As she came closer I realized that the darkness of her skin was scar tissue, and somehow I knew that she had been burned at the stake. I went to my studio and decided to paint what I had seen. I did two paintings of faces with flames coming up around them. Each time I made sounds as I painted and seemed to look through the woman's eyes, watching the people as she burned. She kept saying, "How can you do this to me? I am your friend." This was so startling that I put the two paintings away for almost a year. I felt fear and caution. One day two dear friends were doing a painting weekend with me and I showed the pictures to them. "Something important is going on here, Barbara," one of them said. "I think you should be open to what is being asked of you."

Then early one morning I woke up hearing a voice in my head saying, "There once was a time, a horrible time, there once was a time, a horrible time, there once was a time, a horrible time." This phrase continued to repeat itself. I turned over to try and go back to sleep, then suddenly sat up and said to myself, "Get up, Barbara, something important is happening." I went to my computer to write down those words. Line by line, word by word, a story was given to me of a woman who had been burned during the Inquisition, the "Burning Times"–a

300-year period starting before 1500 AD, when people with power, wealth, wisdom, and healing skills were killed in order to eliminate competition with the powers that were beginning to establish control in the cities.

This woman was the community midwife, healer, and herbalist. She worked in relationship with angels and nature spirits, who revealed to her the herbs and healing methods that would be best for each person who came to her for healing. She became a target of fear and was burned by her community of friends and neighbors. As it turned out, she didn't die; though badly burned and vision impaired, she was determined to remain a healing agent in her community, saying, "I will not let what happened to my friends happen to me. I will not let fear control me." Unknown people left food at her door, and slowly she healed enough to take action. Her heart ached for her friends, so each day she sat at the community well and hummed the songs they used to sing together, to heal them and herself.

As I wrote the story, I began to see paintings I had created decades earlier. This was such an amazing experience that I

Guiding Angel

became frightened and concerned that the subject matter would upset people in a way that would affect me. I put it all away for a couple of years and didn't show it to anyone. But I couldn't forget it. So I decided to put the story with the pictures in a three-ring binder.

The gnomes then asked me to write what had happened to them when, during this time, most of their human partners were killed. I was so frightened, I was not capable of writing their story at that time. Finally, years later, I felt an urgency to create a real book. I was still very cautious and only put one paragraph about nature spirits into the book, *The Burned Woman*, published in 2001. Now those subliminal fears have been healed and I want to make it up to Mano and my Council and pass on their request of humans.

A huge hidden fear, I have come to feel, resides in the collective unconscious–the fear of persecution for being different. I have heard a number of people say, "People will think I am crazy if they know I hear voices and see auras." I believe there is a fear within the collective memory that people with inner sight and hearing–those with spiritual connection–will be considered crazy and removed from society in one way or another. Writing *The Burned Woman* became a tool for my own healing, which I am told released a healing energy into the collective consciousness. But my angel told me to realize that people's fear of the nonphysical world, and even their fear of their own intuition, is the result of personal experience or fear left in the collective consciousness when 15 million people were killed for their spiritual gifts over a 300-year period. Today's ignorance of the reality of angels and elementals, plus people ignoring their own spiritual gifts, may be the result of personal fear originating in the Inquisition.

THE STORY'S INFLUENCE EXPANDS

After publication of the book, I felt guided to create a workshop focusing on healing those who have memories of the burnings or fear being different. I tried a variety of ways and found the easiest was to create a DVD, *Healing Burned Woman*, essentially a reproduction of the book. When that was finished I heard the inner voice, which I now know was Mano, say, "You have told Burned Woman's story; why not tell your own?" And so I created another chapter–"Barbara's Story." With that complete, Mano said, "You have a lot of messages from the Council; why not tell 'Nature's Story'?" And so I did. Then, once again, he reminded me that Jim and I and our

Burned Woman DVD

friend, Hope Peal, had spent ten years creating and presenting a program for Conscious Living that I could easily adapt as a workshop for presenting the Burned Woman material. That became the fourth part of my *Healing Burned Woman* DVD.

The workshop, in which I present the stories and follow the guidelines the DVD offers, has been a blessing to many people through the years. I have presented it in my home, showing part of the DVD before dinner and the rest afterward. The table conversation is always stimulating, and the evening is a lovely way for friends to share. The largest group I have had so far is twenty-four, and it still worked. Each person went home with an awareness about themselves and a commitment to bring change into their lives and their personal worlds.

Mano encouraged me and gave me the confidence to publish *The Burned Woman* book and to create the DVD *Healing Burned Woman*. Later, as he brought me to the Council of Gnomes' work in the new studio, he guided me to paint always within the consciousness of this Council. Still further on the path, as I became more adept at seeing and hearing in the realm of nature spirits, he set me to transcribing the messages and conversations I had become a part of. Under his guidance, this led to establishing a blog that brought our experience to a larger audience. He wanted others to become aware of how a human can work with a spirit of nature on a regular basis, in a co-creative adventure.

Earlier Mano had encouraged me to create a small book on messages from the Council of Gnomes. I was just beginning this project when Jim died. I put it aside for a number of years, making a few starts but completing nothing. Then I was totally let off the hook when he suggested I invite Mary Jane Di Piero to collaborate on a blog with him and with me. This beautiful offering has been going for nearly five years now. I live in gratitude, respect, and honor for the role I have been able to play and the blessings I have been given.

As with my gradual understanding of how Mano and Rama entered my life at various points to nudge me toward my current level of work with them, information about the burning times also filtered in through the years. During my 1948 bicycling trip in Europe, for example, in a large city in Belgium we visited a torture museum. I didn't know what it was about, but looked at what was called "the rack." A person was tied to this wooden structure and a large round wheel pulled the feet in one direction when the wheel was turned. Another round wheel at the top pulled the body in the other direction. Next I saw a metal case like a mummy, which opened up for someone to be placed inside. I noticed spikes inside that would go into a woman's breast, belly, and pubic area. In the basement I saw small cages where people were kept. I didn't know of the burning times and didn't think too much about it, but these memories returned over and over through the years.

My awareness of the burning times increased through another traveling experience in Europe, this time with Jim. A hill outside of a town, the Witches' Hill, had a stone at the bottom called the Witches' Stone. The story goes that a woman suspected of being a witch was put into a barrel and rolled down the hill. If the barrel hit the stone, it was proof that she was a witch and she was killed. Although the women who did not hit the stone were proven innocent, some of them died simply from fright or from crashing down the hill in a barrel.

Those times have passed. What I see happening at this time, in my life and others, I name as residue from the Burning Times within personal memory or memories held in the collective consciousness: fear of the unknown, fear of the nonphysical world, fear of accepting and acknowledging personal spiritual gifts. I have seen myself and other women expressing fear of stepping forward as women of power, due to fear of persecution or ridicule.

The times have changed. The call is out for each of us to be the fullest expression of our divine nature, so that we each contribute to the better world that is promised as we move into the Seventh Golden Age.

The World of Faerie

PART FIVE

THE WORLD OF FAERIE

MY FIRST AWARENESS OF A FAERIE CONNECTION came in 1988, soon after I moved to the Mountain. I was taking a series of three workshops with Joy Gardner, a Santa Cruz author teaching from her book, *Healing with Color and Crystals*. The second workshop was held in a small cabin high in the Santa Cruz Mountains. Joy had invited her teacher Swami Ti, a man in his mid-60s, to come and teach with her. I liked his teaching and felt comfortable with his gentle way of speaking and being. At the beginning of the second day he told the group, "There is a woman present who speaks with her hands as she shares in the group. Her hands," he went on, "speak the language of Faerie." At the end of the workshop, when I said goodbye and thanked him for his teachings, he looked deep into my eyes and said, "You are the lady who speaks with her hands. You are a Faerie queen and your hands tell their own story as you speak."

At that time, my only familiarity with the word *fairy* was of tiny ladies with butterfly wings and flower dresses. I couldn't imagine being one of these, so Swami Ti's comment confused but also intrigued me. I decided to go into neutral, not to accept or reject what he had said but simply to hold it in the palm of my open hand with the prayer, "Dear God, reveal to me that which I need to know."

THE TEACHINGS OF R.J. STEWART

AT THE TIME I WAS UNFAMILIAR WITH THE WORD F-A-E-R-I-E—a race of beings living in the nonphysical world and known in

Celtic history as the Elder Race. They lived within the etheric level of earth, a little higher than human and a little lower than angel. A major step forward in solving, or maybe even deepening the mystery of Faerie came when Kyla, my gardener, loaned me R.J. Stewart's book *Power Within the Land*. R.J. is Scots, a carrier of the lineage and teachings of British mystics and the magician W. G. Gray. I had connected with Gray 20 years earlier when studying the Tarot. Most of the books I had found on the Tarot were so esoteric that they left me more confused than enlightened. The owner of the metaphysical bookstore I ventured into in Hollywood told me of a new book he thought I would like, written for people just learning about the Tarot's mysteries rather than for deep scholars.

R.J.'s book, *Power Within the Land*, like his teacher's, was easy to understand. I was interested to hear R.J. say that he continues to learn directly from the powers within the land and, in his workshops, helps others experience this personally by leading them into meditation journeys. I immediately wanted to attend one of these workshops to see what I might experience and learn about Faerie. Though they were offered in England, I put out a strong wish and intention to attend one someday. Within the year, Kyla told me that R.J. would be teaching a workshop in Bonny Doon, the town next to mine. This was too good to be real, and Jim and I signed up right away. I was surprised to discover, then, that I had a lot of fear, not knowing what I was getting into—an unconscious fear of the unknown that I now believe is a remnant of the burning times and also rampant within the collective consciousness. I had totally forgotten my stop in Edinburgh some years before to visit the gardens and perhaps meet Pan, and how I had become literally sick with fear of the nonphysical world. Now, once again, that feeling arose within me.

When I walked into the meeting room, I saw a stocky, middle-aged man with long white hair and a beard. He had a kind expression on his face and I felt him to be a warm-hearted gentleman. He caught my eye and walked over to meet Jim and me, saying, "I am R.J. Stewart." All of my fears immediately dissolved and I felt comfortable, safe, and curious. I study with R.J. to this day, more than 20 years after that first meeting. He teaches through a lens of tradition–time-honored patterns that evolved over the centuries–working with the powers of the four directions, the energies above and within the earth, and using chants to create certain forms for relating with the Faerie beings. I have had two magical experiences in which the image that appeared in R.J.'s guided journey was one I had painted many months or even years earlier. In these ways I became familiar with the Faerie tradition and teachings, and realized the connection I had already made through my paintings.

In his book *The Living World of Faery*, R.J. says that soon we will enter directly into the "living world" and find that we have come home. The Faerie tradition is for everyone. It is a spiritual way for ordinary people, a source of spiritual wisdom and ancestral lore, and a way of communion between human and other living creatures, both visible and invisible. It is not a religion, but a way of relating. There are also major cultural and environmental differences, for the shared properties of consciousness have

God of the Mountain

to filter through the lands, the planetary zones, the people. The Faerie tradition is about relating to the life in the land. Each land and location is different.

ELLIAS LONSDALE AND FAERIE

My astrologer, Ellias Lonsdale, was most helpful in my growing interest and understanding of the world of Faerie. Ellias had talked with me about his own personal experience with Faerie beings, and as he read my chart he encouraged me "to be open, to explore, and to allow" the contact I was beginning to notice when I entered the Amphitheater. In 2003, Ellias lived in my guest cottage and at that time was impressed that the Faerie realms were coming closer to humanity and wanted to interact with humans on a whole new level. His Faerie contact told him that "all of the Faerie realms could arise in their new harmonic" within the Amphitheater.

When I asked Ellias how he experienced Faerie, he described being in a remote, incredibly beautiful spot on an incredibly beautiful day and feeling completely in tune with Faerie. He said there were certain spots in Hawaii where he felt that same sacred magical energy.

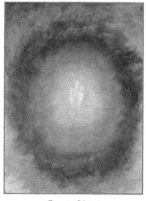

Faerie Blessing

"Sometimes, if I am very open to it, I will experience the Faerie realms in a particularly fine-tuned way like a circle of light and colors moving around me. My part is to be in the center of the circle, to acknowledge what is there and be with it. The most prominent multisensory impression is of being with a lot of bright, vibrant, youthful beings who are so much more at one with the planet than I am, who want me to join them, and who recognize me and want to give me back to myself. They perceive that humanity is really caught up in the mind and they want to infuse human mentality with a vision and vibrancy that spins us beyond our mental blanking of everything around us so we can open to Faerie in a natural way. The Faerie tradition is simply itself—a set of customs and practices preserved orally through the centuries in Western and Northern Europe. Faeries are living beings that are one step, one change of awareness, beyond humanity. Western culture demonstrates our flight, our rejection of the subtle holism of living beings. It began with the propaganda of state religion, in which the older deities were decreed to be either evil or no longer valid.

"Before the fall from grace," Ellias said, "Faerie beings were the elder brothers and sisters of humanity. When humanity went on a divergent path, it could no longer tune into or interact with Faerie, so Faerie had to take increasing responsibility to hold the earth and the elements intact. They had to be the preservers and maintainers. Eventually that became stagnant for them." Ellias perceived that I was "being inspired and called to participate in various ways with the liberation of the Faerie realms. The Faerie beings are reaching out to humans who are sensitive and open to the nonphysical worlds, saying, 'We want you to come to yourselves, to come out of the morass that collective humanity is caught in. We want you to lead humanity forward because we can't go on any longer the way we have been.'"

In essence, Mano said the same thing to me in 2003, the first time he communicated with me while I wrote his words on the computer: "We can no longer go on alone. We are in deep need of the nourishment we receive from interacting with the human kingdom, and you are in deep need of us to sustain your lives by interacting with nature. We want humans to trust their own inner visions and feelings of the subtle world we live within."

Ellias laid out three levels of Faerie:

- *Green Faerie* includes the gnomes, elemental consciousness, and nature spirits who live on the surface of the earth, building all we see within the green and growing world.

- *Brown Faerie* includes the great majestic beings who live deep within the earth, holding the structure of the planet stable. These are sometimes named the Gods of the Mountains.

- *White Faerie* includes the beings who live above the surface of the earth, within the magnetic pull of the moon. I think of them as angels and devas.

FINDING MY OWN WAY AMONG THE TEACHINGS

How do Mano and the master gnomes fit into the realm of Faerie? My Council of Gnomes has told me that it has representatives of all levels of Faerie. "Many of us come from dimensions above White Faerie and below Brown Faerie. We are, however, primarily teaching you to relate with the spirits of the land, gods of the mountains, giants of the land–those in the green world. We also have introduced you to an order of elementals that you have named the companions or workers. Their task is to find ways of helping humans live with more ease, opening them to interactions and relationships with another dimension of nature. When you think of the three realms of Faerie with love, a golden presence as bright as the sun flows to us through your heart/chest center. This nurtures us more than you can realize. You always have this presence about you whether you know it or not, yet we receive an amplification when you direct it especially to us with intention, purpose, and love."

The way I see it now is as a work in progress. As Mano says, my spirit and nature teachers always give me a lot of experience before they help me grasp the larger significance of the teachings. They can only teach me with what I have in my mind. Something entirely new, like the thought of having had lifetimes in Faerie, takes a while because I must overcome my antipathy. With the burned woman story, for example, for years I could not understand that many people's fear of nature is sourced in that time.

All of those I've learned from have their own access points to this Faerie realm and its history. R.J. accesses it through traditional rituals. Marko Pogacnik comes to it through his own unique experience, as do Ellias Lonsdale, Machaelle Small Wright, and Rudolf Steiner. The same is true for me.

An understanding and articulation of my path to an acceptance of Faerie and my role arose in me one recent morning as I arrived at the Amphitheater. The Ascended Masters, I remembered, call humanity the I AM race. They tell us that we did not come from another planet but from the heart of creation in the great central sun, out of the union of love and light, out of the union of father/mother god, reconciling the polarity of the infinite, eternal I AM PRESENCE. The individual I AMs are those who *know* themselves to be individual, who can say I AM. The impersonal I AMs were created to supply all that the individualities would need. My perception is that the impersonal I AMs are the elemental beings of earth, air, fire, and water—the four elements that are the basis for all the material world.

The excitement and opportunity flowing through the I AM race was the opportunity to be part of Gaia, a new planet. This meant stepping out of the fifth dimension into the third dimension, to learn to work with solid form. The original mandate rested upon cooperation and constant contact with angels and elementals, who came first to prepare a physical form for the I AM race. The Father/ Mother God, however, gave the I AM race free will to work as it wished, toward its purpose of lifting this third dimensional planet to the fifth dimension, where all originated. The angels watched over these creational plans and held the pattern of creation for the elemental beings to fill with third dimensional substance.

Angelic Protection

This experiment was to take three million years, or three golden ages in time. At the end of the second golden age, the I AM race, perceiving that the experiment was proceeding quite successfully, kindled the desire to separate from their I AM presence and take charge, on their own, of the task of physical mastery. They separated themselves from their God source, their I Am presence and divine plan, and began a grand deviation from original purpose.

Following this fall from grace, people's hearts were hurting. Their antidote was to disconnect from the heart, from the Mother's love. For the first time the planet experienced selfishness, greed, fighting, and killing. The mind took over. The ego, whose original job was to record everything that happens, out of the record of what had gone before, felt concern and stepped forward to guide the lost race. The polarity of light and love, father/mother god that brought perfection, wholeness, and wellness into life experience now turned to duality, pitting the forces of light and dark against each other and bringing discord and degradation.

Some did not participate in the folly of separating from their god presence but maintained their growth and movement from third to fifth dimension—maintained their commitment to serve, cooperate with, and remain conscious of the elemental and angelic kingdoms. My awareness, during this "downloading" of information at the Amphitheater that morning, was that those who did not deviate from original planetary purpose are those I am now calling Faerie. The Celtic historians call them the Tu ah ta de dana, the children of Dana, the Sidhe, or Mother Earth. The Faerie race stayed with their mother Gaia, living within the etheric realm to assist those of their brothers and sisters who took the perilous path away from polarity to duality. I am calling this commitment, to remain present and assist with the awakening of humanity, the path of resurrection. It requires the protection of the elementals and cooperation with the angels, seeking their assistance and giving them permission to intervene, since God's mandate was not to interfere with the free will of the people. They cannot do anything for us unless we ask.

I see that this story has been unfolding within me since 2004, when I first connected with the Ascended Master Teachings. Yet it could not unfold to this point of awareness until I had accepted my own role as Faerie Queen of the Amphitheater, in service to Mother Earth, in union with Joseph and Jon. (More on Joseph and Jon below.) I live in constant gratitude to the Council of Gnomes, my elemental teacher Mano, and my angelic teacher Rama, who have led me step by step from my first soul awareness to this huge story within my own small life.

THE FAERIE MYTH THAT RUNS THROUGH MY LIFE

For three summers, from 2014 to 2016, I dedicated two to three months to my work in the Amphitheater and studio, calling these my "summer journeys." At the end of summer journey 2014, I began to come to new realizations about my lifelong connections with the world of Faerie, particularly in relation to Joseph, whom I had encountered through Mano not long after moving to the Mountain.

What has caused me to open, finally, to the world of Faerie and my role in it? My earlier hesitation came from a lack of knowing. When I arrived on the Mountain I had little solid experience with other realms of being and still doubted my own intuition and perception. The 2014 summer journey helped me relax, with trust, into a new reality. Thus, when I encountered the warm, good energy of Joseph and the "brothers", I trusted myself enough to engage with new possibilities, and to open my mind and heart. I signaled that Joseph could start stepping forward and gave him a door to walk through. I had changed. After that, I often saw Faerie beings in the studio, mostly men in soft indigo shirts and pants, and I remembered that off and on during the years I had seen them intermingling with Council of Gnomes. I was learning to accept them.

When I wrote *The Burned Woman*, I was afraid to share my growing relationship with the elementals and the spirits of the land. Now, wondering what to say about Faerie, I have been tempted to travel that same path and postpone writing about what I see in glimpses will be my next major involvement and interaction with Mother Earth. Instead of taking the path of fearful avoidance, however, this time I have resolved to share the pebbles dropped along the way that lead me to more information, more experience, and more knowledge. I will hold Mother Earth's directions in my heart and let her lead the way. When I know what I am doing, what I am about, I will write another book, or share my new findings in the Council of Gnomes blog. Meanwhile, as I complete this book of living with the spirits of the land, I will share what has led me to this point, drawing an arrow that will carry me to a deeper relationship with nature and my love of the planet.

The concept of Faerie is a thread of mystery that has woven itself in and out of my consciousness through information dropped into my lap from people, books, and inner awareness. As I look back, I see that incidents I gave little thought to in the moment coalesce into a picture over time, a beckoning toward the future. For example, sometime in the mid-1990s I was led on a journey into the earth. It started on the forest side in front of my studio and I walked underground, following the same path I walked to the Amphitheater each day. I ended up in a large open space under the Amphitheater filled with pale green light. I felt the presence of beings but without clear details or memory. I now call this a Faerie temple and later learned how to journey directly there. It was usually set up as a sanctuary with seats leading to the front, where I met the Goddess of the Amphitheater, the Green Lady, Mother Earth.

Another entrance is a hole between the roots of one of the Amphitheater's "Sister Trees." Mano invited me to enter the hole and follow him down the stone staircase. A light at the bottom showed different directions I could go. This is very similar to one of the guided journeys R.J. leads. Mano turned to the right, where a tall thin being in brown with a long gray beard seemed to be the guardian of the doorway. He looked at me with a sweet expression and said, "Greetings, Daughter." Mano and I entered and walked down a long aisle to the east, which seemed to be the front. The same pale green light permeated the space. At the front of the temple I met the Goddess of the Amphitheater sitting on a small dais in a large chair. I knelt in front of her, put my head in her lap, and cried, calling her Mother.

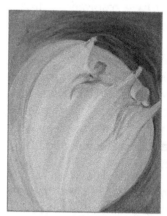

Twin Flames

Jon came forth around 2008, on a journey to the Goddess in the Faerie temple. He faced me and held my hands, and I immediately felt a deep love for and from him. I had not seen this being before in my lifetime, yet I knew him; he was so familiar, and we shared such love. It was as if I had come home to God. I don't remember if we spoke that day, but he kept appearing. After years of loving interaction and guidance, one day I received the information that Jon could be called my "twin flame". This concept was comfortable yet also quite unfamiliar to me. As always, I simply held the new idea in my heart and asked for the truth to be revealed. Mano later gave me a big-picture view of Jon's role in my life as twin flame.

It began when our God presence became aware that the small planet Gaia was prepared to take inhabitants who wanted to learn and to create in third-dimensional form. Starlight, the name I received for my God Self, had met Gaia and wanted to participate. Starlight herself stayed in her fifth-dimensional home base but sent forth two parts of herself to enter the third dimension. I, Barbara, came to the physical dimension of the planet; Jon also came to Gaia but lived in the nonphysical dimension. His job was to be ever present to guide and support my exploration. It can be said that he carries the Christ consciousness, while I carry the consciousness and duality of the third dimension.

In the summer of 2017, the first day I accepted and owned the role and title of being the Goddess of the Amphitheater, Jon stepped inside of me and became part of my body and of my inner life. This seemed very comfortable and correct. I have a place in the center of my chest bone that always feels comforting when I place my finger there. When I touch that spot, my energies ground into the earth and I am in the presence of Mother Earth. That has become Jon's home base inside of me, the "golden sun's presence", a small sun there in the center of my chest. He offers wise council and constant companionship when I connect and ask questions.

Further Travels to Discover Faerie

In 2000, when I entered my "earth studio", I saw a door I had never seen before. Curious, I entered and saw a small gnome sitting on a throne. He said he was equivalent to a king in the Faerie realm, and that he would like to travel with me on the month-long trip Jim and I were taking to a Findhorn conference on angels. The conference organizers had used one of my angel paintings for the brochure. After the conference, the being said, we would go on a tour of sacred sites to the highlands and islands around Scotland. There were things he wanted me to experience. I said yes, and off we went.

Jim and I spent a couple of nights in the Chalice Well Guest House when we first arrived. As we walked the garden we came to the Chalice Well; its water is red and its source is unknown. It has never gone dry or diminished in volume. The gardener asked us if we would like to go into the well. Once a year, they block the water and clean the well for a sacred ceremony celebrating summer solstice. I climbed down a ladder and stood in wonder at this amazing opportunity.

On Orkney Island I had another opportunity to go deep into the earth. A Neolithic site had just been discovered in a farmer's yard. A hole in the ground went down around 10 feet, then took a bend with a cut-out place that looked like a bed and went down 8 feet more. I was the first in our group to go down and one of the first fifty people to enter since it was discovered. My Council says this was an initiation and a gift; they wanted me to physically feel space inside of the earth, since I enter my earth home by traveling through my consciousness. A few years ago, I met a man who told me he had a home in the ocean. I have wondered, since I have been introduced to my home in the earth, whether every soul has a home in one of the elements; perhaps some people have homes in the air, and others have homes in the light, the sun, or fire?

My trips to Scotland, Ireland, and England in the early 2000s (four trips in four years) were essential for connecting to the Neolithic parts of myself. Now I have come to see that these experiences were leading me to my Faerie heritage and inheritance. My opening to the Neolithic came after a vision of a stone briefcase. I was sitting on the bed in my guest room in the vision, and someone was taking the briefcase away from me. I yelled, "No! Stop, that's mine; I'm the carrier of the lineage." The briefcase was like an anchor, opening me to recognize my original connection and experience with the stones. I followed the stone briefcase to Neolithic times.

In Ireland, at Loughcrew, for example, the familiarity of my hand touching the carvings on the entrance stone brought tears. I sat inside the cairn and cried and cried, then came out and lay on the wet grass with light drizzle falling on me, still crying. I closed my eyes and had a vision of a tall man in a white robe lifting me onto a stone altar. He pulled out a long, thin knife, about twelve inches long, and pointed it toward my heart. I became alarmed and called, "Rama, Rama is this okay?" My body relaxed and I said to the being, "If you are going to take out my heart, I want you to give it to Mother Earth." He replaced my heart with a star. Later I shared this experience with Ellias, who asked, "What kind of a star was it?" I realized that it was not the Star of David with six points or the common five-pointed star; it had seven points. "A seven-pointed star is a Faerie star," Ellias said.

Recently another pebble was dropped into my consciousness, remembering a visit forty years ago to hear Torkom Saraydarian speak on the Ageless Wisdom. I carried one statement from his wisdom sharing that filled my heart with longing and became a constant theme within my prayer life: "to become a soul-infused personality." The new revelation is that meeting the Faerie beings on my land is soul work. As I accept my role within this race, my personality will become infused with Faerie consciousness and my forty-year prayer to become a soul-infused personality will be fulfilled.

Faerie Temple

Blessing on My Journey

PART SIX
SUMMER JOURNEYS
2014–2016

SUMMER 2014:
FOCUS ON SPIRITS OF THE LAND

THE LAST DAY OF WRITING CLASS, 2014, my teacher Carolyn Flynn said, "Today I want you to write about your plans for the summer journey you will be taking." My yearly trek to Mount Shasta had been canceled and I had no plans to travel. My mind went to the year-long journey Jim and I had taken to Europe in 1985, and I wrote about the personal transformation I had experienced that was instrumental in moving me from San Luis Obispo to the Mountain in Ben Lomond. Thinking of the Amphitheater and the beings of the land I now regularly relate with, I decided to create an adventure, to take a summer journey from my home to the Amphitheater every day for the months of July and August.

The spirit of adventure filled my heart as I entered the Amphitheater the first morning of my "summer journey." My first stop was to lean into the Mother Tree and say hello, and then to say hello to Rama and Mano and to the beings of the Amphitheater who were present. Discussing this adventure with Mano, I found he was full of ideas for me. The major one was to connect with the spirits of the land by choosing a stick from the ground and then, using India ink and white paper, to let the energy of the land flow through my body, through the stick, and onto the white paper, making marks without thinking–just marks. Each day I found a new stick and let it talk. "Each stick has its own personality and voice," I was told. I would open my heart to the land, put the stick in the ink, and let the marks flow onto the paper, with no thoughts and no control, just letting it happen and watching what came forth. I felt the work going on deep inside me, drawing out aspects of myself as I followed the stick over the paper. Then I opened the computer and looked

with my inner vision to see if anyone was present. If I saw no one, I would ask, "Does anyone wish to speak?" and would record what happened on that day. Sometimes I stayed for 15 minutes, sometimes for 4 hours. I sang spontaneous songs and at times became aware of energies around me, or of thoughts forming in my mind.

Day after day I followed the same routine, day after day I detected a different energy, day after day I felt totally blessed—just like on the year-long journey Jim and I took to Europe. By the end of this summer

Ink Stick Drawing

journey, I was a different person. I was softer inside, more whole, more sensitive to the spirits of the land. I was in love with the Amphitheater, with Mother Nature, and with life. I was blessed. I feel I was bonding with the land in a new way—always sitting on the ground, always opening into an expanded heart space, always giving the amount of time needed to come to a conclusion. I experienced being truly in love with the land as I worked from the energy in my heart. The ink-stick drawings were a road map into the inner nature lying below the surface of my mind and intellect and above my conscious feelings. I would simply observe as the stick guided my hand, rather than my hand guiding the stick. A vast open space opened inside me that took in all of the land and atmosphere of a particular area.

In order to expand my being to encompass more than I often connect with, the nature spirits had to do something to move me beyond my comfort and knowledge spaces. The "little drawings" (described in Part Seven) couldn't do it because they are so familiar. I've done them regularly since the 1970s, and they often have a purpose—such as calling for transformative action to heal a situation.

One day toward the end of this first summer journey, as I entered the Amphitheater and greeted the Mother Tree, she said, "Sit down, my dear, and talk with me." I felt so much love flowing to her, and I moved into gratitude for the information and gifts given in my daily summer journey travel. "I love you, dear Mother. I am so grateful for the clarity that has come during this summer journey." db. The Mother Tree responded: "My desire, as you come to be with me and with those who live here and are learning to relate with you ('their human'), is for you to sit with your heart open and your mind clear, tuning in to any information or sightings you might perceive."

I took my nap at the base of the Mother Tree and woke feeling a circle of 12 master gnomes around me. Behind them were tall flame beings. I did a drawing with a stick that I found in the bark of the Mother Tree. It had very light lines that dropped dots of ink, and the drawing ended up with an eye in the center. In gratitude I said, "I feel so expanded, deep and soft. I send blessings and gratitude to all who live here and all who visit. Out of my heart flame I send the threefold flames of love, wisdom, and power up, through, and out—out and out to all of nature and the forces of the elements." Suddenly I felt words form in my mind, "That is very good, little lady. You received and followed directions very well." I felt a being a little behind and to my right, in the area I call the Giants' Knoll. "You need know no more," the being said. "only that we are watching and approving of what you are doing."

Summer Solstice Celebration

My daily summer journey pilgrimages to the Amphitheater wove around other activities that grace this sacred space, such as the Summer Solstice celebration conducted by a group as a yearly dedication to a life of service. The morning after the ceremony I wrote: "It is early Sunday morning and today's visit to the Amphitheater needs to be short so I can be ready for my day. All of the decorations are still up and flying after last night's Summer Solstice celebration. The group who performed the ceremony comes each year after a week at Sequoia Retreat Center, next door to my property. Colored banners are flying, and each chair has a different colored cloth representing a

Solstice Celebration in the Amphitheater*

season. The ceremonial center—a live tree in a large pot—signifies the group's tree of life focus for this ceremony. Mano is here to greet me and tells me that many spirits come to participate in the celebration. 'After the humans leave,' he said, 'we enter for our own dance, ceremony, and dedication to Mother Earth and her transition from past to future. This happens at each turning of the wheel of seasons.'"

Joseph of Faerie

As my 2014 summer journey came to an end, I started noticing five human-sized men walking to greet me as I drove Betsy, my small off-road vehicle, to her turnaround spot. They were wearing loose indigo-colored cotton slacks and jackets, similar to the clothes I saw on Chinese men and women when we traveled through China. I felt very comfortable in their presence and looked forward to seeing them when I arrived. I called them "the brothers". One day an older man came with them; I thought he might be their father. They all carried a warm loving presence. The father was present the morning I made a quick trip to connect and do my ink-stick drawing on my way to the studio to paint. He introduced himself as Joseph, and he asked me to do a special transformational painting in the studio that day.

I sometimes do what I call "kerfuffle" paintings. "Kerfuffle" means a fuss or commotion, and for me that means moving and singing and yelling with wild abandon–as I paint. I do the kerfuffle painting to very loud classical music. The music gets inside of me and does the whirling, whooping, and stamping, and the paint splashes on the paper to the rhythm of the music. An enormous amount of energy is released, and I feel charged and renewed when I am complete. So Joseph asked if I would do a transformational painting, and I agreed. When the kerfuffle experience was accomplished, I went back into the colors and brought what felt like order and harmony into my body and onto the canvas. As I finished I heard Joseph say, "Thank you, my dear, for trusting me." The sincerity of his voice broke my heart.

Very early on, after I had moved to the Mountain, each time I went to Amphitheater a man dressed in a black suit was with Mano. About the fourth or fifth time, he stepped forward and said, "I am your god." I reared up on my high Christian horse and said, "You are not my god; Jesus Christ is my god." And he never came back.

In the beginning when I had the call to come to the Mountain, I didn't question who was calling or what they wanted of me. I only knew the call was to the Amphitheater and so I came every day. There's a tradition in Faerie (which I knew nothing about) that the father of the family is called the god and the mother the goddess. From R.J. Stewart, I also learned that in ancient times a goddess was a human who interacted with a specific earth location. I didn't know I had been called to take on the role of Goddess of the Amphitheater. I acknowledged holding the energy of the Amphitheater, yet I turned away from the term goddess. My Tarot readings often indicated that the Empress was calling me. I thought it was a call to go to Amphitheater, not to be or carry the energy of the Amphitheater. Many times, however, when I had readings with people, I would say, "I mean to go to the Amphitheater more often," and they would reply, "You carry the energy of the Amphitheater wherever you go."

I was good at following instructions (for example, "I don't need you in San Luis Obispo any longer; I need you on the Mountain") but when I got to the Mountain I had a lot of fear about stepping forward. I received the story about the burned woman so that I could begin to comprehend the culture's collective fear. I needed a big teaching to get me lined up, though even then I was afraid to put the burned woman story into the world. It was a deep fear. I have only recently realized that the kerfuffle painting with Joseph was clearing my old antipathy and gifting me with acceptance.

Until the 2014 summer journey, I didn't know that Joseph and the man accompanying Mano earlier were the same being. I finally saw how eager he was to connect after so many lifetimes—lifetimes in Faerie, not as humans. I see now that I have lived lives in Faerie and I wonder if we are meant to integrate Faerie and the human race as we move into the next age. I just don't know. "I am your god" meant "I am your carpenter, plumber, teacher"—simply that he was my partner in this special place of the Amphitheater.

SUMMER JOURNEY 2015: FOCUS ON THE MOTHER

IT WAS ESTABLISHED at the end of the first summer journey that I would come again the next summer to continue this dedicated daily time in the Amphitheater. These journeys have created a more intimate relationship with the spirits of the land, a deeper connection and commitment to Mother Earth, and a clearer understanding of my soul purpose and life path than would have been possible if I had continued my characteristic way of relating with the Amphitheater, even with my 7,000 visits in the previous twenty-seven years.

I recently found a paper written in April 2004, on my first visit to the Amphitheater after Jim's death and the call for "the real Barbara Thomas to step forward." That day I received clear guidance that, ten years later (which would be after my first summer journey, 2014), I would finally begin to truly understand and embody my destiny. I wrote: "When I connected with the Mother Tree, I could feel a difference. I asked her if my energy had dropped so low because of dealing with Jim's death. She said it was not low energy I was feeling; it was just different. I had been focused on outer things and her energy turned toward the inner. Then I felt a download of energy with a teaching and an assignment."

"Humanity has become so separated from the spirit world," I recorded. "We have become insulated and isolated from the inner dimensions of life, from the divine guidance and nurturing available to us. It is my job to connect, to reestablish the original connection I had in past lives. As I do this, the door will open for others to do the same. All of the Mother's children need to come home."

Whereas the first summer journey focused on feeling the energy of the land and doing ink-stick drawings of different locations, the second year I was asked to focus on the Great Mother, to embody the energies of Mother Earth and add water to the ink-stick drawings to represent her aliveness and love.

The Mother's Womb

I promised myself that I would go to the Amphitheater daily. One morning I didn't have time to stay, so I simply leaned into the Mother Tree, merging inside of her for three or four seconds. When I stepped out of her and moved away, everything in the Amphitheater looked different. I was no longer aware of me looking at the Amphitheater; my vision had grown soft and inclusive. I was not separate; I was part of this space.

Another request for this summer journey was stimulated by reading David Spangler's book, *The Sidhe*. Sidhe live in the dimension of Faerie, which has a higher frequency than the third dimension in which humans live. It was important to the Sidhe that David's group create an etheric standing stone circle, and Mother Earth asked me to do the same. When I entered the Amphitheater the day after I had created this etheric stone circle, I had forgotten that I had done it. As I walked into the center, I felt a strong energy that surprised and confused me, until I remembered. That circle is now a permanent marker protecting the center, or heart of the Amphitheater. Mano tells me that this center is now one heart, one womb of the Mother.

During the summer of 2015 I continued to do ink-stick drawings every day, but the change from the previous year (aside from adding water) was that on some days I was given specific directions. One day Mano said, "I would like you to attune to the Mother. Walk into the standing stone circle and then enter the womb of the Mother. Do not put ink to paper until you feel her presence, even if it takes a long time; be attentive to the feelings." After the drawing I realized that the stick I was using spoke with a sweet, gentle voice. Another day I couldn't find a stick on the ground to draw with, so I used a rolled leaf. "I love it best," I thought afterward, "it creates a more sensitive picture."

Other Children of The Mother

Mother Earth made it clear that in this time with her I was to interact with others of her children who also live, work, or connect regularly with the Amphitheater. This opened me to a new dimension of spirit beings. "Although you have named us 'Amphitheater beings'," one of them told me, "we are from many different races and levels of consciousness. We each have our work to do here, for all the earth. We come here because Mother Earth is present in this place in a special way. I give you just enough information for you to recognize the vastness of brown, green, and white Faerie. Today as you do your drawing, connect with Mother Earth, feel her presence arise and enfold you." My ink-stick drawing was circular, and it felt good, with a pleasing starburst created when the ink hit the water spray.

Another day, as I settled into the quiet, I felt presence around me and, as I had been taught, asked, "Does anyone want to speak?" When someone said, "I do," I responded: "I greet you in love. I don't recognize your energy." The being identified himself as one of the Lords of the Flames of Venus (whom I was familiar with from the Ascended Master Teachings). From the background, he was helping the beings from Venus who were working on Earth. "I have not spoken before today," he said, "though I have been watching you for the past month. I had heard of this work but was not involved until the Empress of Venus sent out a request for more help. Venus volunteered to be guardian to planet Gaia after humanity's fall from grace. She sent her firstborn son, Sanat Kumara, to the planet to discern what needs to be done to protect Gaia and her people. Ages ago the Amphitheater was chosen as a landing spot for the Lords of the Flames of Venus to enter the earth's atmosphere to do their work."

"Much is happening on deep and high levels," the Venus being continued. "I will work with my brothers as long as the work is of interest to me. When I saw that the small group working here on this small parcel of land carried a powerful aura of rose pink light, I was intrigued and decided to come. I see you as a woman of great power, struggling with your humanness and yet opening to vast dimensions and ascended power. I looked at the plan and record of the work here and see that you are on the path of resurrection to reverse the program of the past and return to the time when you were conscious—a long time ago in your octave, and not so long ago as we calculate time. I would like to simply watch you for a while. May I have permission to return and observe what goes on here?" I asked for a moment to go within and ask those who guide me, though I trusted the lords and the empress and knew they would not have allowed this being in if it were not for the good. After my moment of checking I responded with assurance: "I received 'yes' on all levels; please return as you are called."

Walking to the Amphitheater another morning, I saw shadows moving and the image of a large head formed out of the shadows on the driveway at the bend in the road. "Hello, my dear one," I said in greeting. "I have never seen you before." This being replied, "You have not been here with the sun shining like this; I rarely get to show myself and have never been seen by a person." When I asked if the being wished to say anything about itself, it replied, "I don't know how to differentiate myself from the All; I just am."

"Do you have a focus, a purpose, a job, being at the turn in the road?" I asked. "I just watch and am not prepared to talk," it said, as I thanked it for responding at all. I could see many faces as the sun moved over the forest; on a tree trunk there were four faces on top of each other, the noses prominent with eyes above each nose, like a totem pole.

Love Exchange

To express love seems to be the most important interaction a human can share with nature, with the planet, with the gods, and with the beings of the elements. They tell me that having love flow through a human nourishes them more than we can realize. I always have the presence around me, they say, whether I know it or not. They experience amplification when I direct love and purpose toward them with intention.

One morning as I sat in silence in the Amphitheater, I heard a voice say, "Come to nature often to receive your infilling of our love—not our personal love but the love of the Mother. As you walk in nature and receive the Mother's blessing, the love you give back to us is multi-dimensional because her love merges with your own consciousness or personal I AM presence and we receive both. The love and appreciation you send to us on your own is a weak monotone compared to the rainbow we receive when you are filled to overflowing with the Mother's love. Another awareness I would share with you: Sitting on the earth without consciously identifying and connecting, without saying 'Hello Mother' and feeling the energy exchange, is a real loss of opportunity."

Little Ones and Their Maria

On another morning, I was sitting on the ground drawing a face I saw in a nearby tree. As soon as I finished, I felt a group of little ones nearly two feet tall in front of me. As I sat on the ground, we were looking eye to eye. I asked who they were and received the answer, "Keepers of the land–the ones who do all the work around here." Then I felt a woman coming from the west, wearing a full skirt, resembling, I thought, a nanny for the little ones.

My thought was quickly rebutted: "That is not accurate, not so. We need no nanny. She is our Maria and teacher, helping us when we are confused–for instance in how to relate to you. She explains some of your actions that make no sense to us, telling stories of what it is like to be in a human body and to live a human life. It all seems so complicated to us. She says you have more 'chips' inside of you and that they are not all going the same direction. We have only a few chips inside of us but they all work together in harmonious direction and action."

Barbara and the Little Ones

I thanked the little ones for sharing and asked if they wanted to say more. The next day in the Amphitheater I reflected on this conversation. "For my chips to be in alignment means I am open to be a channel for God to flow in and through me, to embody my presence. The elementals who spoke yesterday have fewer chips than I do, yet they are all aligned to allow the God energy to flow through." I looked up and felt the little ones in front of me again. "I am very interested in our last conversation about our chips. I am beginning to understand," I said.

"Then why didn't you do the aligning?" they asked. "Were you conscious of the flow running through you?"

"No," I replied, "but I will do it now."

"True, it is never too late," they said, "but this is what we don't understand. It feels so good to live in alignment. Why would you choose to do otherwise? This is what we ask our Maria, and she says it is a misuse of God's gift of free will. You can choose to remember or forget. We do not have that choice. We are always open, and actually we prefer it that way."

"Thank you for sharing with me. I find your words to be very wise," I said.

"It is easy to be wise when our chips are aligned with the God flow," they responded. "This is what we want for you. Practice here and then take the knowledge into your daily life and interactions. We cannot enter your work or your understanding when your chips are not aligned. You know the feeling. You have found the way to being heart centered many times. Each time you do a bodywork treatment you end up with that 'certain feeling of alignment' where the chips are all going the same way and bringing through the God energy. 'Abiding in the Mother' will also create this state."

On another day at the Amphitheater I wrote: "The way I feel, my chips must not be aligned." I took a deep breath, opened to Mother Earth, and asked her to work through me. All I wanted to do, though, was lie down and close my eyes. I wondered, "Is this in order?" An answer came from somewhere: "There is no reason to do anything unless your chips are aligned." I looked up to see the little ones in front of me. I also felt a presence, like that of the Maria who mothers the little ones.

I heard her voice: "I wish to speak and connect with you. It means so much for my little ones to see what you do and when you pick up their antics and presence. My name is Maria; I am mother to the little ones." db. She continued, "When you work with the beings of the land or another aspect of nature, the Maria, the Mother's love, will always be present. The green land carries this energy, as do you."

Then Rama spoke. "Please hear what is being said, Barbara. We want you to know that you are one of the Marias for this land. Here you feel the heart call to open and be present. When I say open, that means open your consciousness to be aware of the nature beings present in that moment, where you are. Radiate your golden sun's presence with the pink heart of the mother and the love, wisdom, and power flames of the father to penetrate, stimulate, and nurture those who appear. This is an aspect of the glory and grace you are being asked to carry at all times, for all who are near."

"I am grateful for this teaching," I replied, "and I am ready to take a rest. Does anyone wish to speak at this moment?"

"We would all like to say something," I heard. "We are the brothers and we have been waiting for our opportunity to connect closer than we were able to do last summer. We, the brothers, are part of the 'crew' that you, as one of the Marias, watch over. Even though we are all of the Faerie race, you at one time in the long past were our mother, and thus we still think of you that way. We come forth to say thank you and to give you some information that we see you do not have. In our experience of you as a Maria, we see a constant flow of the gold/pink aura flowing out from you and embracing each of us as we receive the first touch of this energy. We see you as a source of strength, wisdom, power, and most of all empowerment. For as we touch in close to your aura, we grow strong within ourselves. There are other ways we connect with you, and it is as if a flame reaches out from you, like the tongue of a dragon. It touches our auras and ignites us with that gold/pink radiant energy. We will sit in guardianship over your body and energy field as you rest."

When I sat up, Joseph was present. I heard him say, "This has been good. While you were resting we were able to remove a big chunk of human and replace it with Faerie energy."

Journey into the Faerie Temple

In a continuing recognition of my position as Goddess of the Amphitheater, Mano invited me to take a quick trip to the Faerie temple beneath the Amphitheater. I went to the entrance under the tree trunk and from there we walked down the stone steps and turned to the right to enter the Faerie court, which felt full even though I did not discern activity. Following my familiar path, I walked up the aisle to the front and saw the goddess off to the right. Chairs were set facing each other, like at a conference table, though I didn't see the table. I heard a voice: "You are perceiving correctly, my dear. I, Joseph, called this meeting. The goddess is here in her etheric presence. I invite you to step up on the stage and take her seat. I will sit across from you and connect through the energy field that surrounds both of us. The goddess represents Mother Earth in this location. As the Goddess of the Amphitheater, you have been chosen to be her representative in the physical. Ruth Prescott and Kay Ortmans both held this position, yet they were so focused on the outer they hardly knew this. Kay had to make a living, and Ruth had a vision to fulfill of creating her school of higher consciousness. You have had all of these needs cared for and you have been willing to follow Mano's lead, and years and thousands of connections. Abide in this, your heritage."

One morning I wrote to the trees, "I love you and am so grateful for the opportunity to be present with you on a daily basis. Today I am feeling the presence of the mature redwoods and madrone trees. They are so majestic, so strong. I feel silent blessing flowing to me."

Words formed in my mind, a response from the tree voice: "I would like to speak. I want you to know that your daily presence this past month has helped to awaken our sleeping energies. To have you, a person, come and just stay here with us over and over, tuning in to the Mother and sometimes actually melding into her presence, means more than you can know. When you do this for one it goes out to all of us. What we are creating here is nature and human spending time together, just the way it was in the beginning. There is much for you to gain in consciousness about our connection, and what you do know is enough for now." I thanked the being and added, "I have the feeling the voice I hear is all of the trees, not just one spokesperson." It replied, "Yes, we speak, live, and breathe as one."

SUMMER JOURNEY 2016:
FOCUS ON THE SACRED FIRE

MY THIRD SUMMER JOURNEY WAS TO FOCUS on the sacred fire and the rainbow rays that flow within it. Different rays come from the sun to bathe the planet with a specific blessing, governed by a specific being and angels of the day. The great cosmic being Amud ha Esh governs this sacred fire.

This year I used colored India ink to do my art, calling in the angels of the day to work through the drawings. As I moved into the third month of my summer journey, everything went along as usual; I drove my four-wheeler Betsy from my house to the Amphitheater, leaned into the Mother Tree to greet her and ask for her blessing, then unloaded my sheepskin to make the ground softer, and my portfolio with papers, basket with stick, ink, water, and snacks. I walked through the etheric standing stone circle, opened to the direction of the angels of the land and the little ones I have named keepers of the land.

I asked, then, to connect with whoever wished to speak and immediately heard a very strong, clear, loving voice say, "I have been waiting for you to notice. I am Amud ha Esh. I desire to work with you on a regular basis for the next few weeks. I will review what has been accomplished as we go and fine-tune the work each day." I didn't end up noticing any change after this encounter and felt that perhaps Amud ha Esh had not come to teach me anything so much as to observe.

One day as I sat facing the north, I saw a Council table in front of me, a distance away, with six or seven energies present. I couldn't tell who they were, though they seemed to represent the layers and levels of beings I have related with here in the Amphitheater over the years. "We are the beings of the land," they said, "this land and many lands. All have direct access to this land. Remember when Una Nakamura came here to do healing sounds each month for three years? When she was visiting in an Orthodox church in Russia, she recognized the same energy as she felt in the Amphitheater. You also connected the two energies while on the Tor in Glastonbury, England."

A lot of ideas began to flow through my mind, suggestions for new projects and for another book. The Council continued, "We are pleasantly surprised with the information you have picked up out of our consciousness this morning." Actually, I couldn't take credit for this ability, since I could perceive the presence of Mano and Rama standing beside me, guiding and directing my interaction.

Mano and Rama allowed some of the Amphitheater beings access to my morning practice of working with the Tarot in order to give them a language of conversation that will be understandable to me when they later speak. I realize that "to speak" means to project images that I pick up and put into my words and understanding. This is the way my friend Fred Kimble communicates with animals when he engages in conversation with them.

"Oh thank you," I responded, "I am so grateful to be a part of this wonderful communication and learning today. I feel it is time to leave now. Is there anything else that needs to happen?"

Rama suggested that I "sit in silence for a few minutes to absorb and integrate the information and energy of this experience. Open your heart to receive, to raise your vibration and open more channels of awareness between you and those spirits of the land that have come today."

SUMMER OF 2017:
MOVING INTO FUTURE WORK

I HAD BEEN TOLD THAT 2016 WOULD BE THE END of the summer journeys, that I had completed what was desired. For approximately 200 days over the three years I had gone daily to the Amphitheater each July and August to make ink-stick drawings and record whatever appeared within my inner hearing or vision. Although I had fulfilled the Council's original purpose, however, I spent the summer of 2017 in much the same manner, going regularly to the Amphitheater and my studio, living in expectation of new guidance for the future.

I continued working on the color ray of the day, using colored inks, and I also started painting again with the sacred rays as inspiration. In one of my dreams, a gardener who miraculously heals ailing plants said, "I just wrap them in rainbows and they get well." That is my work too, with the nature and angelic and human realms.

Gifts and Grace

The Council has often told me, "We do not intend to lose you this time." And so once again, during the summer of 2017, they had to intervene to prevent me from stepping off of the path of love and returning to the old human habit of ruminating about a grievance through criticism, condemnation, judgment, blame, and gossip.

Around 6:00 in the morning, returning to bed after a snack in the kitchen, I fell and fractured my right wrist. I crawled back to bed and bathed my wrist in witch hazel for two hours before I phoned my son to take me to Doctors on Duty. The gift was to stop me in my tracks and impress on me the seriousness of the subtle pattern I had fallen into for a few weeks, ignoring inner guidance and letting outer forces take over. The grace was that I had absolutely no pain and that the cast was small, lightweight, and comfortable. I could even choose colors and so wore a blue cast to match the predominant color of my wardrobe.

During this time of recovery, the Council took me on a deep review of my past, showing me patterns of dysfunction I have engaged in for years. This called for considerable self-forgiveness and deep apologies in meditation to those I have wronged in the past. It really does not matter how small or subtle the incident was for the other person. For the integrity of my spiritual path and commitment to love, each incident was major.

Another gift of insight I received during the summer journeys took me back to earlier events. Around 1990, early in the first of my three bouts with pneumonia, Jim dropped me off for an appointment with a new acupuncturist. As the acupuncturist treated me, he told me that I needed to go directly to the hospital. I told him I didn't intend to do that. "If that is so," he said, "then don't come back to see me."

As I sat deep, deep inside of myself, waiting for Jim to pick me up, I heard the inner voice say, "Barbara, are you willing to die?" I thought about it and replied, "I always expected to live to be a vibrant 80-year-old. Yes, I am willing to die if I have completed all I came to do."

After a short silence, the voice completed the question it had put to me, saying, "…so that I might live." At the time I didn't understand the significance of the communication, but now I know it to be from my God Self, Starlight, asking if I were willing to die to my old, limited being in order to fully live.

*p124, "Solstice in the Amphitheater" painting by TurtleWoman

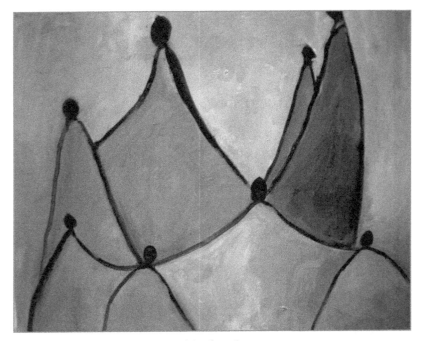

Joint Council

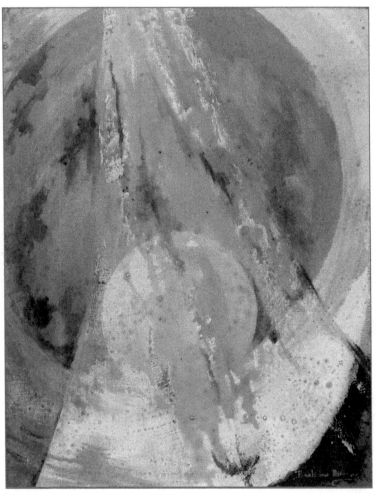

Recurring Themes

PART SEVEN

RECURRING THEMES
GUIDING MY LIFE

TRAVELING THE WORLD AS PREPARATION

WHEN I DECIDED TO GO TO MY FIRST CFO CAMP in 1961, I thought it would be a one-time thing, but the Council had other plans for my relationship with that wonderful organization. In one capacity or another, I participated with CFO yearly for more than 30 years. Actually, I don't think the children would have allowed us to stop going, they each loved it so much. This was a marvelous bonding experience for our whole family. Even though we each did our own thing with our own age group, we ate together, sang together, and slept in the same tent. So much love was present that we all came away with an added degree of wholeness.

When Jim was elected president of the international CFO (CFOI) in 1987, we traveled for three years, two to three months at a time, visiting CFO camps, offering leadership in some of the camps, and always doing a workshop for the Council Ring members on how to create a camp using their own members for leadership. We also taught the Council Ring how to make decisions through prayer and how to speak with authentic language. This meant telling your own truth, instead of using the editorial "we" or "you"–using "I" messages to name clearly what each person's truth is. This teaching was very difficult at first, as it was so foreign to the way different cultures naturally spoke. Soon we started reading about "consensus agreement", which is the same thing we were teaching about making decisions through prayer. By the fourth year of teaching this concept it was much easier, and I felt we had been seeding the collective consciousness along with the ones teaching consensus agreement. At this same time, Hope, Jim and I, and four to six others were using all of these components of the program to create Harmonikos, a teaching for conscious living.

In CFO we taught that when a decision needed to be made, each person would go into prayer and ask god for a *yes* or *no* answer. When the count was taken, each person would silently use a thumbs up for yes, down for no, or sideways for a question. Next would come a discussion to clarify the question, and then another going within to listen for the answer and make another "thumbs" report. Almost always, the unanimous answer would be found by the third round. If this didn't happen, we would table the question until the next day. A magical thing would happen during our time apart, and the solution would appear.

These travels were very hard on my body and I needed to take a day of rest after each three-day workshop. I needed time to myself to go within, read, meditate, sleep. Jim, however, was hale and hardy and ready to travel with our CFOI friends to see the wonderful sights in their area. I did a lot of little drawings of the energies of the lands we were visiting, mostly using a calligraphy felt-tip pen—a great tool for drawing landscapes.

Once I sat behind the driver while riding in a public bus in the Philippines. The wooden sides rattled, making a huge noise. Looking over the driver's shoulder, I could see dogs, pigs, and children crossing the road in front of the bus. The driver never seemed to slow down, only swerve around the things blocking his way. I was terrified until God gave me the thought: "This man wants to live as much as you do. Sit back and let him do his job."

God spoke another time, while I was riding a public metro underground in Japan. Jim and I were standing holding on to a strap and the sleek train roared underground, rising to the surface at each stop to take on the next group of passengers. At one stop around 30 school girls and boys flooded into the car, chatting and laughing with one another. All of a sudden I was filled with fear. I felt foreign, strangely different than these children all dressed in blue, all with black hair, all with dark eyes. I was different and I was afraid. I prayed and God said, "Perfect love casts out fear, Barbara." And so I opened my heart and sent love, poured love to the whole group and to each individually. At this point we came above ground to pick up a passenger waiting for the train, a tall blond woman. My first response was that she looked very different, even strange. Then I realized, "Oh, she looks like me." And I realized that in sending love to the children, I had identified with them and lost my self-consciousness and my fear.

Nearly 30 people joined together for a week-long camp within a compound in India. Adults, teenagers, men, and women moved together in the unity the CFO program creates. One afternoon I stepped outside the compound and started to walk toward a small group of teenagers I thought were part of our group. When I felt their caution on seeing me, I realized these were not the teens I was relating with inside the compound. I offered a prayer of gratitude for the opportunity to share God's love, acceptance, and friendship with the ones on the inside of the compound walls, whom I had been with all week.

I would say these years of traveling into other parts of the world left me with a knowing that love unites strangers and builds friendship. The adjustments I had to make in myself to be comfortable wherever I went, whomever I was with, whatever I ate, wherever I slept, formed a constant, all-encompassing prayer, a prayer simply to remain unshakably comfortable.

Jim and I did a trial run of a training manual being created to share with the overseas campers, so they could learn the program, the process, and the pattern for moving from one part of the program to another. It was designed to move from inner to outer, or right brain to left brain, over and over during the day, and the program was the same every day. The camp ended with an experience of wholeness. I have seen this work for one day, a weekend, or a 7-day camp; it is true magic and wonder.

I traveled with a laptop computer and a small printer to be able to print new information and instructions that came up as we were teaching. I believe it was the singing and body movement, and the creative aspects of the program that held the participants together.

Once we presented a four-day camp in Hong Kong, when a missionary requested that we come to serve "his people". I thought we would be working with missionaries, but "his people" turned out to be recovering drug addicts living in a small abandoned fishing village in a cove at the foot of high cliffs. It was touching to see how proud those men were of each other when someone would share what they had written or drawn. Their prayers were so deeply sincere that my heart cried

God's Angelic Care

for them. Two other leaders were Dr. Kim from Korea and Jessie Bano, an elderly woman from Japan. Jessie came in a white suit and "stable but fancy white shoes." Her sweet love and concern touched the boys' hearts, and as we left she had at least three young men helping her walk up the steep dirt path out of the cove and back to our waiting cars. Jessie thanked the boys and told them God had given her the 23rd Psalm as a promise of protection and safety on her journey. The verse says, "God has given his angels charge over thee, to guide thee in all of thy ways." She named the boys her angels.

These trips opened protected, closed places of comfort within my heart and mind as I constantly adjusted to what was present before me. I learned how important it was to remove the dust of the day, as well as to wash my eyes, ears, and nose each night to get the literal dust out. I became comfortable going into public toilets where both men and women would take turns going into the closed toilet closets. I found how important it was to "ground myself" in order to stay in my body, to release opinions and judgments, and to be in constant alignment with God, sending forth prayers to prepare the way and giving myself permission to take a nap.

All of this adjusting to new experiences, new people, and new lands involved learning to trust God in all things. I see this as excellent training for my later work and the beings and experiences waiting for me when I moved to the Mountain. Seeing Mano walking beside me the first day was not as unfamiliar as seeing men in Papua, New Guinea walking around the streets in loincloths with feathers in their wild bushy hair, or the women in Bali with breasts uncovered and a cloth wrapped around their hips.

I have often wondered that I have walked on the land of 53 different countries around the world and have driven through every state in the United States, including Hawaii and Alaska as well as Puerto Rico. I don't yet know the overarching reason for such travel. Someone, however, sent me an astrological birth chart with lines over a map of the world showing the places my soul was familiar with. My chart did not have half a square inch without a line. I have seen a couple of other charts that had wide open spaces and a lot of lines collected in one or two countries.

I have had experiences in India, Scotland, Ireland, France, China, and the Philippines where I have recognized and identified places I know I have been before. My take on this—and the fact that so many people are traveling the world, participating in time shares, touring in large groups (like the Japanese factory workers who, every five years, are able to travel with their colleagues to some new country)—is that the soul returns to familiar places, either to pick up energies left behind or to release trapped energies no longer needed. Some place in that awareness is the call of the Seventh Golden Age, for each of us to become free within our consciousness and move on to be the fullest expression of our larger self that we can possibly be. Two outstanding experiences on trips to Chartres, France, and Goa, India indicated that I was returning to a land and location in which I had once lived in another time.

In 1985, while visiting the magnificent cathedral at Chartres, France, after walking around looking at the carvings and the stained-glass windows, I walked through the chairs set up in the main sanctuary. Looking at the floor, I had an amazing realization that I was familiar with the stone pattern in the floor and felt I had been a nun in this church. I opened my heart and asked, "What kind of a nun was I?" The answering thought was, "You were the stern and sturdy Mother Superior." As we continued our tour into the basement, I noticed a dried-up fountain dedicated to "sturdy souls".

Our last trip to India, in 1991, was centered in a Council Ring training and retreat in a Catholic monastery in Goa. One day we took a quick tour of the area and entered a lovely Catholic church. We walked through the main hall, went downstairs to pass through a sanctified area where the bones of the founding priests were stored, then went out into a garden of beautiful flowers and greenery. As I got back into the bus, I was shocked to discover I didn't have any energy; I was so drained I could hardly climb the stairs into the bus. I went to bed as soon as we got back to the monastery and asked, "What happened to me in that church?" The story flowed through my mind that I had been one of the founding fathers in that church, very dedicated to God and not very loving to the community of worshipers. As I walked past the bones that had been my body, there was a release of energy that had been trapped there. By morning I had my energy back and felt that the soul of the priest had been set free and, I hoped, had grown more loving.

SQUIGGLE DRAWINGS

LONG BEFORE I CAME TO KNOW MANO in person, he guided me into the experience of doing little drawings while traveling or in meetings. During our vision quest traveling, I began drawing the energy of the cities and sites we visited. In Paris I was surprised to see that the drawing had the shape of the Eiffel Tower; in London it had circles that reminded me of Trafalgar Square. Seeing this, I intentionally focused on drawing the energies of the angels of each place as we traveled. As I did the drawings, I began to sense the potential inherent in the process. This practice continued and deepened when I started doing small squiggle drawings after Jim and I joined the CFOI board in 1977.

My first experience in this context was when the leader talked and talked and talked, hardly ever touching the point. I was bored and did the drawings to entertain myself. As he went round and round on a certain subject, I saw myself drawing lines that went round and round. I then made a powerful direct line to the center and scribbled a tight energy. At that point the speaker got to the point of his circular ramble and we were able to move on.

Transforming Oil Spill

In another meeting there was discord among those trying to reach agreement. My drawing was strange and discordant. I then used soft lines and color to bring harmony to my drawing. The discussion among the participants also came into harmony and agreement. After a week I noticed that all of the drawings I did of one particular speaker were three shades of blue. I began to notice other similarities and realized I was drawing the energy of the people as they spoke. A woman sitting beside me noticed what I was doing and commented that my drawings almost exactly matched the auras she was seeing.

While living in San Luis Obispo, I worked for a healing clinic doing color clearings for individuals. This entailed having them draw the energy of the story they had been telling me. I then turned the paper in each direction to see if they could find another picture or see a way to enhance the drawing. The insights they had and the transformations they made to the drawing would create a release in the individual's body, heart, and mind. I have done this for myself for years and always find a release and change in myself, and often in the situation.

I have done hundreds, if not thousands of these little squiggle drawings. The purpose is to give a form to the formless, either to see what is present or to intentionally create transformation in a difficult situation. When the form is clear, it can be identified and changed if necessary.

Mano led me to discover that the drawings I do in nature have a very special purpose and service. Once while at the Grand Canyon as I was drawing I heard the inner voice say, "This will help Mother Nature to see herself." On a family vacation in Yosemite, camping by the river, I painted the magnificent granite Half Dome. When the work had been on my wall for a month or so, I saw an elemental face in the cliff. I knew that I had painted and revealed the spirit of Half Dome. I think my "cultural deed" in this instance was to give this spirit a way to be seen, and perhaps a way to see as well.

When doing a pencil drawing of a face I saw in the bark of an old redwood tree, the face kept changing. I drew the next face that appeared, the next, and the next, until the light shifted. Mano explained that when the elementals making up the tree realized I was drawing them, each lined up for a chance to be seen. I was pleased to be able to give the elementals an opportunity to be acknowledged by a human. They hunger and yearn to return to the old times when people interacted daily with the elementals, in their houses, yards, and neighborhoods. Mano often tells me that a simple "hello" helps to restore what has been lost.

I constantly use the little drawings to release my own pent-up energy, frustration, fear, or anger. I deeply focus on the feeling in my body, then pour that energy onto the paper with strong lines and feeling. Sometimes I yell as I do the release. When I feel the energy subside, I then transform it by going back into the drawing and filling in spaces with color. This often reveals to me images or actions that create a picture, which then transforms the energy I have put into the squiggle. My changes to the drawing thus change the energy in my body. I always feel a release and a return to harmony.

Over and over, Mano says, "Your little squiggle drawings are your most important service." He often asks me to do a daily drawing to release and transform energies in certain world situations prominent in the current news. Anyone can do this; it is a doodle with a purpose, and as the lovely saying goes, "Try it, you may like it."

Around 2003, the gnomes told me, "Our request is for you to look through the newspaper and find an article that strikes you. We will bring things to your awareness, and then you make little drawings of the energy you feel from the article. Open to healing the situation and transforming the energy within your drawing." After doing this for a couple of months, I was quite amazed at the results. Mano told me that these drawings were my service to the earth–janitorial work as a conscious human being to help clean up the toxins other human beings had left behind. "Now this, Barbara, is truly one work that you can do well, easily, and effectively. Much is accomplished in these little drawings, so enjoy the process with great gratitude that your prayers have been answered to be of service and make a difference in the world."

One specific request the nature spirits made was to capture on paper and help transform "chaotic energies alive and flying around the planet." Mano said, "What your government puts up for self-protection has boomeranged to hold in and ricochet the fear and chaotic feelings people are expressing. This is escalating beyond all belief and the potential outcome is very dangerous. We are calling on many to work in their own way to clear the force field of the flying thought forms. We would like you to capture some of these on your paper and transform them by giving them to Mother Earth. This is work that you can do with pencil, pastel, or crayon–whatever is simplest for you in the moment."

INTERACTING WITH ANGELS

BEFORE I KNEW THE REALITY OF THE PRESENCE OF ANGELS and was just beginning to believe they were real, I was sustained by the Bible verse: "God has given his angels charge over thee to guide thee in all thy ways." Then synchronicities and coincidences began to occur. A book about angels came in the mail from an anonymous benefactor. I met Patricia, a woman who interacted with angels on a daily basis. The angels asked her to come to my house weekly for almost a year to work with me and help me "wake up." Patricia taught me that since God has given humans free will, the angels cannot intervene in our lives unless invited. She taught me to call in the angels each time I saw a need, read the newspaper, or remembered at a concert or public gathering to invite the guardian angel of everyone present to come close and give a special blessing to its person.

Angels started appearing in my abstract paintings. One of our babysitters, Maria, was able to see the nonphysical world and was a constant source of information about the angels she saw when we prayed together. I have learned that we each have many angels assigned to us, and each one establishes a method of recognition or communication with its person.

While Jim and I were in Europe in 2000, I visited Dev Aura, the home of AuraSoma healing oils. I participated in a meditation in which amethyst stones were placed around each participant. In addition, I was given a crystal to hold in my hand. As the leader guided us into a journey, my soul took me on a journey of my own. I saw myself as an angel flying with a number of other angels carrying Gaia, our planet, through the sky to set her in the perfect position within our galaxy. The teacher was very impressed with my vision and gifted me with the crystal I was holding, saying it held a "library" of experience that would open its knowledge to me some day. As often happens with me, I was mystified, wondering how this could be true, so I simply held the mystery, waiting for understanding to be revealed. Years later, listening to an Ascended Master Teaching, I learned of a birthing place in the galaxy where new planets were being created. This would take eons of time, and when the planet was ready a special angelic transport would deliver the planet to its home base.

At another time, the Ascended Master Teaching again opened my awareness. A bulletin went out from the Great Central Sun announcing that a new planet, Gaia, was ready for inhabitants. Anyone in the fifth or higher dimensions who wanted to experience living in the third dimension, to learn to create with physical energy, could volunteer. The experiment was to take three million years, with the goal of raising the individuals' and Gaia's energies from the third back to the fifth dimension. They were to be called the "I AM" race. I had the awareness that my soul, my I AM presence, volunteered for this adventure. She had admired Gaia's courage in volunteering to host inexperienced beings by giving them a space in which to learn to work with third-dimensional energies. I felt my presence send a part of herself to participate in this experiment and in some way to protect Gaia.

A few years ago, when my vision first diminished and I was not yet sure of myself, I flew with two of my children to Portland to participate in a grandchild's wedding. My children were not used to my having physical limitations and walked ahead, excitedly talking and looking for our rental car. I found myself at a cross street with cars exiting the garage and became scared, unsure of my safety. My children were too far ahead to call for help and no one was around to ask for assistance. So I prayed, "God help me." Immediately I was aware of a large being on either side of me. Together we stepped into the crosswalk and all of the cars stopped as the three of us walked to the other side of the road. These beings stayed with me until my children were in sight and I knew where I was going.

Once I was speaking about angels at a week-long retreat. A man came up to me afterward and said something like, "You have to be careful of evil angels." I don't know what kind of lies he had been listening to; I only know that God is love and the angels are in service, messengers of God.

We each have many angels assigned to us. The delight comes when a method of recognition or communication is established. Some angels communicate with me by giving me a sudden prompting nudge to take an action. A certain feeling, a deep involuntary breath, is confirmation and affirmation that my current thought is accurate. Sometimes I hear a bell or inner sound. I always think an angel is present when a synchronistic event occurs.

Sometimes I create an inner spontaneous dialogue to find out what is happening. The thoughts are so fleeting I can easily miss them; I have learned to create these conversations on the computer, and then I remember and learn. To connect with your Guardian Angel, take time to find her name, and use it often–visualize, ask. Light a candle with a bowl of water in front.

In 2017, with all of the turmoil going on in the world, I was asked to give the angels permission to come in when I turn the light off at night and the angel light shines bright through the ivory screen I had purchased on a trip in 1985. My prayer is something like this: "Come, come, come all of the angels. Come to protect innocent people, come with solutions to our world problems, come and do whatever you can to stop destructive people and keep our world safe. I thank you. I love you. I bless you."

When we ask, angels will go before us and prepare the way for our safety, success, and beauty. In this American Indian prayer, I enjoy visualizing "beauty" as "angels".

May I walk
May it be beautiful
May it be beautiful before me
May it be beautiful behind me
May it be beautiful to the right of me
May it be beautiful to the left of me
May it be beautiful above me
May it be beautiful below me
May it be beautiful within me
May it be beautiful all around me
May I walk
May it be beautiful
In beauty it is ended.

ORACLES

IT IS MY BELIEF AND EXPERIENCE that everyone on the spiritual path needs an oracle—an outside source of information that gives guidance and answers to specific questions, or a new perception and clarity on what is happening in daily life. Ancient cultures created a way of divination to discern the will of the divine. I have used many oracles over the years, such as the I Ching, angel cards, or the Bible. Jim used the runes. I have finally settled on, and learned to trust, the Tarot and the pendulum.

The Pendulum

My first try in using the pendulum for information was a complete failure—and perhaps a hidden blessing. In the early 1960s I accompanied Jim to Phoenix, Arizona for a business conference. I wanted to use the car while he was in his meetings and when I couldn't find the car keys, decided to ask the pendulum whether Jim had them with him or if they were in the room. I got the answer that Jim had them. When he came back and told me they were in the drawer, I felt betrayed and did not use the pendulum again, because, I said, "It lied to me."

A decade later, while living at Findhorn, I took a workshop with Marko Pogacnik, the Slovenian sculptor and geomancer who uses a fascinating process to create installations with huge stones in parks and public places. He goes to the site, aligns with the land, then uses a pendulum to determine where the installation wants to be placed. He goes to the quarry and has the pendulum direct him to the stone that wants to be used in the sculpture. Back at the site, the pendulum shows him the exact direction the stone wants to be facing in the chosen location. The workshop was set in the huge garden at Newbold House, a small community within the larger Findhorn Foundation.

We were to find a stone and ask, "Do you want to be moved?" Next we were to observe whether the pendulum moved in a yes or no direction (which had already been established). My second rock responded that it wanted to be moved. When I asked the rock to direct me to its new location, I felt the pendulum move in small, straight-forward jerky movements. Then it changed direction and made short movements to the right. As I turned my footsteps to the right it went straight again, and then in a few more feet it went in a circle. The circling told me I was in the right spot. Now I needed to know which side was to be up and how it was to be turned. When the rock was in its chosen all-around right place, the pendulum went in a circle. I became a believer and have used the pendulum as a clear guide ever since. The pendulum had not lied to me in my first and only attempt; I was simply ignorant and, I would say, arrogant. I had not taken time to gain trust in the process.

Interacting with the Spirits of the Land

I use anything on a string as a pendulum. Right now I am using a beach rock with a hole and dental floss for the string. When desperate for guidance, I have often used my car keys, and once I used my shoe, holding it by the shoe string. I always start by aligning with my higher discerning intelligence, asking for clarity. Then I talk to the pendulum to embrace it as a tool for consciousness, and I ask it to give me a yes answer, and then a no answer, to be sure we are in agreement about its response. Anytime I feel things getting "fuzzy", I stop working and come back later to continue the questioning.

The Tarot Cards

Another Council of Gnomes project that I now see was designed to further my work with oracles—as one more way they could connect, teach, and guide me—involved the Tarot. I first heard of the Tarot cards from my friend Brooks when I lived in La Cañada. She once did a short reading for me in which the Fool came up as the one guiding my life. I now associate the Fool card with the cartoon character Mr. Magoo, who was near-sighted and absent-minded but nevertheless always came through unscathed. He might step off a skyscraper into open space, only to step into the empty spot on a two-seater, open-cockpit airplane that was flying by at just the right moment. I can relate to Mr. Magoo's adventures when I acknowledge the constant and consistent guidance, opportunities, and people the Council brings into my life.

I connected with Pamela Eakins' book *Tarot of the Spirit* when I was doing research on the elements. I saw that she was brilliant and had more information than I had seen in any other Tarot book. She offered a year-long course of monthly Tarot classes called "The Fool's Journey", which I very much wanted to take. However, the class was in Half Moon Bay and the commitment seemed impossible during this time when Jim and I were traveling and away from the mountain so much of the time.

Two months after Jim died, I heard that Pamela was going to hold "The Fool's Journey" in Santa Cruz, the first time in 21 years she had offered the class away from her home. I enrolled immediately and loved the teachings and the teacher, feeling as if I had come home to a dimension of myself that had been dormant for eons. To be able to involve myself in this amazing, all-encompassing study during the time I was adjusting to Jim's death was a huge blessing. With my daily homework and meditations, study filled the hours I would have spent with Jim.

At the end of the year, Pamela announced that she would be offering a deeper study of the Tarot at her home near Half Moon Bay. Diana Hobson and I made this journey every month for three years. I loved driving along the barren California coast between Santa Cruz and Half Moon Bay, watching the seasonal changes, the wildflowers, birds, and storms over the sea while relishing the magical and marvelous conversations that always developed with Diana. (Adding to the pleasure of the trip was my personal commitment never to drive by the Swanton Strawberry Farm food stand without stopping for fresh strawberry shortcake.) Pamela is an amazing, articulate teacher, and I admired and appreciated the group of women who gathered for her classes. Our theme was "Becoming a Woman of Power" and by connecting with the energies of each season and developing my artistic abilities through the daily assignments, I was able to focus and articulate much more precisely what I am doing and what my life is about.

In one of these daily workings I stopped complaining to myself about all the work I had to do now that Jim was gone and moved instead into self-empowerment. I am privileged and blessed to live in the heart of the redwood forest where I manage 12 acres of land and a small retreat house. I open my home, studio, and land for people to come live with me for three days and explore the creativity and magic of this place. In the land's natural Amphitheater space, I can cross the veil between worlds and receive guidance from angels and elementals who live on this land and involve themselves with my writing, my painting, and my life.

Oracles Abound

In addition to the above two divination tools that I use daily, I cherish others. A few years after moving to the Mountain, I started studying with Ellias Lonsdale. Every Monday night (when I was home), I drove through the mountains to his little cottage in Bonny Doon. It is only in this writing that I realize I have used my astrological readings with Ellias as an oracle. On each reading, my request for focus has always been the same: "Tell me what the stars are doing in my life right now." Over and over, Ellias presented information that explained what was going on in my inner and outer life. It gave me clarity, comfort, and direction, mostly by reassuring me: You are on the right track, keep going. My connection with Mano, the Council, the angels, and Mother Earth were all seen and named in the stars, and to add to the meaning he could offer, Ellias also worked with the conscious beings in the world of Faerie.

We have now worked together for more than 20 years and I have done at least 50 readings. I am eternally grateful for the Council guiding me to Ellias–the one person I have found who, as a result of his own work with the beings in the world of Faerie, could understand, support, and encourage me to follow my guidance and continue venturing into the world of Faerie with confidence and trust in the larger picture. I want to acknowledge with wonder and appreciation how often the Council arranges for things to be so convenient. Imagine the wonder that Ellias only lived a couple of miles from my home, in the remote heart of the redwood forest.

Another of my most trusted and treasured guidance signs, I now see can also be named "oracle". The Radiant Rose Academy teaches that when a deep, involuntary breath moves through my body, it is the action of the Holy Spirit bringing awareness that what I have just heard, or thought, is truth. In my notebooks I always designate this occurrence with "db".

A further revelation that came through my studies with Pamela Eakins has named and guided the next phase of my life, based on studies I am doing with the Radiant Rose Academy: It is okay to be different, to be guided by a gnome, to work with oracles, to work with a household of small elementals; it is okay to be me, to let the real Barbara Thomas step forward. This awareness made the pieces of my life fall into place and made everything okay.

Using Oracles for Setting My Intentions

I put my oracles, especially the Tarot cards, to work as I set my daily, weekly, seasonal, and yearly intentions. I set an intention for the year, usually stimulated by Akasha's teaching or a project that is coming up. Then I set an intention for each season. I also record what happens in my life on the moon phases: new moon, waxing, full, waning. Moon mother's frequent appearance in my Tarot readings has shown me how very active she in my soul service to the planet. And years ago she guided me to speak to her in a journal with each moon change, which I did for a couple of years.

Each week I set an intention, after I transfer the previous week's guidance to my "subject review" category. Once I set that intention

I lay a six-card Tarot spread as an overview for the week. Then I move into the daily work, which I call my "spiritual practice". Daily I pull three Tarot cards and do a reading on each card. I then open correspondence with my nature spirit teachers, Rama, Mano, Joseph, and Jon, with personal comments on the happenings around the Tarot or in my life. Someone will respond with information, guidance, or comments. Mano recently told me that with this consultation I am actually connecting with the Council of Gnomes–the part that is invested in my personal growth and commitment here in the Morning Practice. When I go to the studio and formally open the Council of Gnomes, I am connecting with a different set of beings who observe more and interact less. They may or may not tune in to the Morning Practice, depending on whether my current focus is of interest to them.

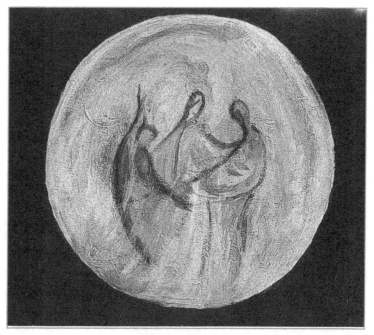

Full Moon Celebration

FROM THE EDITOR

Mary Jane Di Piero

BARBARA, MANO, AND I BEGAN the Council of Gnomes blog collaboration in April 2013. At the beginning we didn't know how it would develop, though we had plenty of material since Barbara had notebooks full of dialogues with Mano, Rama, the Council of Gnomes, and the Faerie world, plus some forays at making these exchanges into a book. Two events early in the blog's launch caught my imagination: Barbara told me that Mano had recommended me for the job of compiling the blog, and at our first "how to do it" meeting she suddenly had the guidance that I was to actually participate in the collaboration, rather than simply editing and bringing form to what she had long been recording. I was charmed to have been recommended by a gnome, and I was cautious about abandoning my anonymity to enter more directly, and accountably, into relationship with the elemental world. Still, I had a belief in and fascination with conversing across realities, and embraced the challenge with surprising surety.

I met Barbara some thirty years ago. At first it was not so much the woman who attracted me as it was the sacred Amphitheater I discovered on her Mountain. It seemed magical, the tall, no-nonsense redwoods mixing with the curved mature madrones, and both supported from below by a sprinkling of deciduous trees and shrubs, filmy and delicate, an interweaving of different sensibilities that allowed a special spirit to filter through the space. Barbara and Jim Thomas owned the Amphitheater and Barbara led sacred circle dances there. Coming from the other side of the mountain, from the jangle of Silicon Valley and the flurry of my daily life, I relished the dancing: simple steps repeated over and over, until my feet knew them and my body could lose itself in the haunting music and the ancient passed-down wisdom of movement dedicated to heaven and earth. And yet, I went to the dances only a few times through the years.

In 2005, when an old friend and I both left Waldorf School of the Peninsula at the same time, we chose the Amphitheater as the place to hold a labyrinth ceremony. With other friends, we laid the Chartres form in forest debris and 1,000 tea lights. After that I started doing small retreats at the guest cottage, spending hours in the Amphitheater alone, in the rain, early in the morning, at night, sitting in tree hollows, gazing, longing, doing my best to honor the energy I felt there. I have always wanted to see angels and elementals, and I knew this must be one of their portals. I had also formed a belief through the years that such clairvoyance or "second sight" was not my gift or my task in this lifetime. Nevertheless, this belief did not keep me from feeling a sense of loss that I had no palpable access to the extrasensory realms I have solidly supported for so long.

On my retreats I would always visit Barbara, and she began telling me about her long-cultivated relationships with the nature spirits on her land. Once she showed me the draft of the Council of Gnomes book she was working on. It intrigued me and also puzzled me: What, in reality, was this new world she was striving to describe? I rather weakly observed that the manuscript would need some editing and that I might be able to help. I was skeptical, since I couldn't see, then, how it could come out of its dreamy fairytale mist into the palpable, practical daylight.

What began to grow in me, however, was the consideration that, like other forms of spiritual discipline, the back-and-forth communication Barbara described was a practice and a process, not a propensity that one either does or does not have. My acceptance that such "bells and whistles" were not for me shifted to questions: Why *not* me? Why not anyone who is willing to do the work? And therefore, why hadn't I so far been willing or able to do the work successfully?

I went down to the Amphitheater after one of these conversations with Barbara and decided to put this new possibility to a test. I lay down on the ground and declared: "I'm not going to leave until I have a message from one of you elementals!" It was a warm day and I loved being there with the sun dappling through the tree branches; I could wait. After a short time, the words came into my head: "Go home and talk to your own elementals!" I laughed, because, indeed, at the moment I was living in an ensouled place myself—another one of those portals—and it made eminent sense to start there. I also acknowledged, with some tentativeness, that my request had been granted, and that it had come from a space beyond doubt.

In retrospect Barbara and I agree that my early flicker of interest—my soul offering to engage with this project—also caught Mano's attention and led him to recommend me, some years later, as blog collaborator. My experience with the blog reminds me of two biblical stories. In my desire to bring the elemental world and its availability to a wider circle of ordinary people, I have often nodded toward the "doubting Thomas" position (Thomas, who wanted proof that the arisen Christ was authentic), in order to address the difficulties and find a bridge to trust and belief. And I have hovered between Martha and Mary in the Lazarus story—Martha being the worker who tended to the practical details of life, and Mary being the dreamer who sat at the feet of Christ, entranced with the new message.

The task of presenting the blog led naturally to the compiling and editing of this book. I see the small pieces of my story that open the blog as embroiderings on Barbara's quilt, illustrating in my own language and sensibility her belief that life, through Spirit, guides us to our destiny tasks. For Barbara, the broadest definition of her life task was to contribute to the connection, once again, of elemental, human, and angelic realms, as our time demands. For myself, although I feel clear acceptance of earlier destiny tasks, this one, this participation in the connection project, has yet to reveal its full mystery. I am following the golden embroidery thread, however, with fascination, willingness, and trust.

Angelic Support

DIVINE PLAN TIMELINE

This plan to work with the Council of Gnomes has guided me from birth.

La Crescenta

- Heard inner voice for the first time: "God is within you"
- Read many books recommended by teachers
- Found little gnome statues

La Cañada

- Was immersed with my family in La Cañada Presbyterian Church
- Began painting with teacher Oscar Van Name
- Attended first CFO camp
- Painted with Minerva Hertzhog: burned women faces, non-objective
- Noticed gnomes appearing in my paintings
- Studied metaphysics with Gene Dorsey; read 100 books in a year
- Attended Hazel Burrow's meditation group; met animal communicator Fred Kimble
- Influenced by Brother Philip
- Studied with Darrell one year: God is both within you and outside of you
- Partnered for prayer and channeled with Maria Dookey, my friend and son's babysitter
- Meditated with Brooks Lewis: Tarot, elementals, collage prayer cards
- Had dinner with Brenda Crenshaw, medium
- Spent three months in Europe with family; 5 years later visited Findhorn
- Met weekly with Patricia Settles, who cleared my aura and saw my spiritual light
- Worked with Olivia Crawford, a psychic who channeled Dr. Ling and introduced me to Rama

- Learned from Marilyn Mudget and Desert Women Singing in the Spirit

- Took High Point classes with Edith Stauffer; vowed to work with angels

- Attended Omega with Cliff and Loma Custer

- Went to Meadowlark Farm and connected with elemental and my earth home

- Visited by naturopathic doctor David Tansley; became vegetarian

- Received chiropractic treatment

San Luis Obispo (Beginning 1975)

- Advised not to join anything for a year to avoid repeating earlier experiences: "Something new is coming"

- Visited by Olivia to help with shock of moving

- Attended EST training

- Did Apple therapy (worked in an apple orchard) with metaphysical friends Evelyn and Ellis Redstone

- Talked daily by phone with Evelyn, who saw me as a "seer"

- Did CFOI work in Australia; named leaving my traditional church to become metaphysical

- Cooked for Loma Custer at week-long retreat; learned to cook without recipes, met dowser

- Moved to mobile home on the ranch

- Had barn-raising party to build studio and workshop; featured in *Sunset Magazine*

- Met Patricia regularly on Meditation Mountain and at ranch; she came to help with Peter's wedding

- Attended art classes and participated in art shows; sold paintings

- Tended horse, goat, chickens, garden, made cheese, canned and dried food

- Learned to weave and spin; sewed ethnic dresses

- Developed new style of dress (tunics, artistic, ethnic); got clear on what styles and colors were true for me

- Jim built house with the help of a carpenter; house designed by Jim Maul

- Experienced death of my parents and all of my aunts and uncles within 10 months

- Supported older children as they left home: Donna went to college, Peter and Donna Sue married, Anne and Steve married

- Had acupuncture treatments with Eliot Cowen, who worked out of my studio once a week

- Did Rolfing with Patricia Wandler

- Participated in Aquarian Energies with Mary Eudora Covington

- Participated in Holy Order of MANS community; meditation and daily communion

- Attended metaphysical classes with Diane Dudley and Jerry Towell

- Did color clearing and energy drawings of people at two psychic fairs on ranch

- Held women's workshops on ranch with Hope Farr, who also offered consciousness counseling after my mother's death

- Participated in weekly Santa Mara women's consciousness group for 2 years

- Held seasonal parties 4 times a year; began to focus on nature and creating community

- Participated in Ken Rose's community consciousness group

- Held community consciousness monthly meetings, which involved singing light opera, joining together in beach and house parties

- Joined CFOI board and leadership; joined Planetary Citizens board

- Attended Planetary Citizens symposium in Toronto

- Hosted Peace Pilgrim for two days

- Started channeling Rama after meeting him on visit to Olivia

- Had regular visits from Vandria Rayner to support my channeling

- Purchased the Amphitheater

- Vision of gnome in the smokestack confirmed by Aunt Katherine

- Bought Hanna and Barney Smead's cabin near Amphitheater

- Traveled in Europe for a year and moved from disbelief to belief in angels, elementals, Divine Mother God

Ben Lomond 1987

- Moved to the Mountain

- Received guidance from the beginning from Mano and Rama; learned to trust them

- Visited and painted in Amphitheater each day

- Worked with Hope Farr and others to create *Harmonikos Program for Conscious Living* with Hope Farr and others

- Hosted monthly circle dance in the Amphitheater

- Attended moon ritual in Amphitheater three times a week for eight months with Mark Borax

- Studied gemstone healing with Joy Gardner

- Had pneumonia three times in three years

- Connected with my God presence, Starlight

- Worked with Ellias Lonsdale, his classes and astrological readings

- Received and wrote *Burned Woman's Story*

- Spent months away from home when Jim became CFOI president for four years; traveled to third-world countries offering leadership training; traveled to Philippines, Japan, China, India, Sri Lanka, Kashmir, Africa, Paupa New Guinea, Australia, New Zealand, Fiji Islands

- Received guidance to resign from Harmonikos and CFOI boards to do my own work

- Bought beach place, 1997

- Worked with healers Helen Jo, Oceana, and Bob Moon

- Began participation with Council of Gnomes, 2001

- Painted angels and elementals

- Completed Yogananda's 3-year correspondence course

- Traveled to Mexico with Moe Ross and BJ King

- Received a blue crystal from Nature

- Attended Kathy Williams' painting class for three years; painted for two weeks in Italy with class

- Joined writing group with Carolyn Brigit Flynn

Ben Lomond after Jim's Death, 2004

- Received challenge: Will the real Barbara Thomas please step forward?

- Traveled to Celtic lands to visit Neolithic stone monuments 4 times in 4 years

- Studied Tarot for seven years with Pamela Eakins' Pacific Mystery School

- Participated in Ubundan Mystery School

- Worked with Akasha Mystery School

- Broke leg; heard "This is a gift, Barbara"

- Wrote *Celebrating the Magic of Jim's Road*

- Created DVD of *Burned Woman's Story* plus *Barbara's Story, Nature's Story*

- Conducted *Healing Burned Woman* workshops

- Collaborated on Council of Gnomes blog with Mano and Mary Jane Di Piero

- Wrote *Living with the Spirits of the Land,* compiled by Mary Jane Di Piero

Mother Earth

APPENDIX:
COUNCIL OF GNOME SESSION TRANSCRIPTS

COMPUTER RECORDING OF COUNCIL OF
GNOMES MEETINGS, 2013

The "db." is my symbol for an involuntary deep breath that signals my connection with the Council.

Barbara: I am not going to the Amphitheater today; it is cold and I have a cold. I will call Council in my studio to keep in touch with my commitment. I see the familiar setting: chairs in a circle and table across from me. I don't see anyone in the speakers' chairs.

Mano: I, Mano, am here. The others are gathering. db. The little ones are arriving and filling in the bleachers. The chairs are saved for the Masters who will be coming today; they are filing in, in procession, as judges entering a courtroom. All are here.

I, Mano, have guided your review of journals yesterday. As I said before, I am always surprised when you do not remember what you are about. Even though I am surprised, I also am compassionate, for it must be difficult to lose home base so often. db. Your prayer to carry the energy of Divine Mother and your commitment and dedication to Mother Earth are the place to start. Whatever you do needs to come out of that number one commitment.

A Master gnome from the right side of the circle comes to the speakers' table.

Master gnome: I would speak. We also watch and see what is happening. Your mind is like a circle; the roulette ball spins around, and your focus lands where it lands. I would be so bold as to suggest that you see the ball as your commitment to Divine Mother, Mother Earth, the divine feminine in you and all humanity. Where she lands is the place into which you pour love and wisdom—it is what comes to you to do. For example, Gretchen arrives in half an hour. Pour the Mother's love on her, as you are holding that sacred space while listening to my discourse. db.

He continued: Yesterday's journal review spoke of pouring forth rhythmic waves of divine love, like the ocean waves flowing to shore. You can name, or qualify, what is to come by sending it out on rhythmic waves of divine love and naming your intention, as you did to find your hearing aid. Now do it again and send it on a rhythmic love ray. That adds the feminine, the feeling of the Mother's energy to your qualifying or naming. It also gives the companions and elementals a sweet energy as they move into place to manifest your request. You will notice it also opens your heart and gives you a sweet feeling. "Sweet" is a word I would suggest you savor: a sweet connection with Gretchen, a sweet time doing dishes and sweeping the floor. db. *Soft and rhythmic energy follows the word "sweet." A sweet time was had by all.*

The Master gnome went on: Thank you for letting me speak. db. I have been observing you through the eyes of the happy sweet gnome that sits on your sink and sings "Welcome home," and sometimes sings, "Come home, we miss you." db. I retire with a word of encouragement. Welcome home. Your life is coming into focus. It will not be so distracted as it has been in the past. (db.) You are in the right place and your presence is ready to come forth. We are all here to assist this manifestation. We sing hallelujah.

Barbara: I thank you, Sir. That was very lovely and helpful. I send you love and gratitude, and to all who have come to Council this day.

Mano: Notice the feeling of expansion and activity in your heart. That is the feeling of pouring love rays from your heart, and this is what you have been "dying" for, waiting for, praying for, to feel love. We also have that need and desire. Actually, everyone and everything has it. How wonderful to have found the way to make so many people happy with such a simple and sweet action. db.

Barbara: I will close now. Thank you for this time. Is there anything else? Then I send rhythmic waves of divine love.

Sending Rhythmic Waves of Divine Love

RECORDING OF A COUNCIL OF GNOMES
SESSION WITH THE LITTLE ONES

Mano: "The Little Ones have some things to talk over with you. We, the larger gnomes, are here to support them. Officialius is in the speaker's chair and will speak for the others.

Little Ones: We are angry, hurt, disgusted, sorry and sad. Does that make an impression on you? You are not paying enough attention to us for us to learn what we had hoped from you. We think you are a wind bag, or a thought bag. You think you are doing the work and you tell people about us, but really you are not relating enough for us to learn.

The Little Ones Register a Complaint

Barbara: I am truly sorry. Truly. I acknowledge my error. Actually, I don't know what to do with you. I notice what you are doing when you catch my attention, like today in the Amphitheater lying beside me, one on each side.

Little Ones: You might ask us what we want to know, what we want to learn. You might consider us as half of this working arrangement and speak to us, not just think you know so much.

Barbara: I can really feel your anger and indignation. I did not want to hurt your feelings. I guess having feelings is a good thing and you can see how unconscious humans can be–how unconscious I can be. Please don't take it personally. I get caught up in my life, what I see in the outer world, and I forget the inner.

Little Ones: That's just the point. What we want to learn is how to wake up a human, how to relate with a human, how to make your life easier so you will know we are here. You could ask for help.

Barbara: That sounds like a good plan. What do you do? What can I ask of you?

Little Ones: You have already met Conrad, who works with computers. When you sit down to work, ask him or just the gnomes in general, meaning the seven of us Little Ones, to assist you with the computer. We are in charge of everything that is physical, everything that has form. You could just say, "Hey guys," and we will be alerted.

The first stage of our relating was for you to get the pictures of what we are doing when you 'look in,' and to see that it relates to what you're doing. This was to amuse you and help you realize that we're real and not in your head. Ugh. There is no room in there. From our perspective, you have thoughts firing off like rockets every second. This day of meditating 20 minutes each hour should show you how little quiet there is in there. Oh yes, I understand it is better than it used to be. But as far as we are concerned it is still very busy.

Barbara: Okay, let's get back to how we are to relate. I truly want to do this. I feel honored that you have come. I want to be trustworthy and respectful of this connection. What can I do?

Little Ones: Ask and see. Talk to us about your wants and desires in the manifest world; we would like to be of service to you in manifesting your dreams.

Barbara: Have you noticed I do not have a clear picture of what I want?

Little Ones: Start with your desire to paint, to create pictures that are healing. Ask us to bring aliveness to your images, to embody the paints with consciousness and inspire the shapes that have power. Yes, this is possible for us. We are also under the tutelage of Master Gnomes who know how to do this. When we don't know, they are always there to instruct us. This is the way we learn to work with a human, by being given an assignment and then seeing what we can do. Conversation would be most helpful.

Barbara: Okay. I would also like to learn to do this. I guess that is the human's part of learning to relate.

Little Ones: You humans have been so arrogant for so long, even those of you who are not basically arrogant act in that manner by default.

Barbara: Okay, let's start. I want to have passion and love for the painting process, to be excited about the exploration, wonder and discovery. I would like you to guide my painting to make sure I stay aligned with the Divine. I want to use color combinations that are stunning, to have a balance of hues and incorporate more white than I have in the past. Then when I am at my desk, I would like to be efficient and speedy—and the same with packing and email.

Mano: That's enough for now, Barbara. Don't overwhelm yourself or the Little Ones. They needed to speak their frustration in a way you could hear. Take each of your desires and let it unfold as you start a particular job. The best time to speak to the gnomes is when you begin a task by creating sacred space.

WELCOMING CELEBRATION AT THE CLOSE OF SUMMER JOURNEY 2016

I arrive at 4:20. So pleasant. I had tried to talk myself out of coming because it is cold in the house. As I stepped out of my front door, I fell over a box that had been delivered and left at the door. I am so grateful that I do so much getting up and down from the floor; I fell gracefully and only gouged the skin on my left leg. I am now nurturing it with witch hazel.

I see the little ones and "their Maria." The thought comes to name them "Keepers of the Land." Jack invites me to journey. I shift my consciousness, bringing Jon forward and Barbara back so I am conscious of our being united. I go to the Sister Trees and meet Jack at the entrance. We start down the stone stairs and I see the light of the landing ahead. At the landing I see Lov-o-lay in his brown suit, with long gray beard.

Love-o-lay: I give honor and grace to you, my dear, as you step one foot forward onto the path of service.

Barbara: Thank you, Love-o-lay. I love you and bless you.

Together we walk through a wooden door like the one in the dream power Tarot deck. Jon is beside me on my right, Jack is on the left, Love-o-lay walking behind. A long line of beings is walking behind him. They are the spirits of the land. Some are very serious and proper, and others are dancing with little skirts swishing around them. These are the faeries.

Faeries: You said you don't relate with Faeries, so we want you to see that you do.

As we walk forward, a full congregation of beings sits in rows on each side. Each row stands as we approach. Joseph is standing at the front, with the Goddess of the Amphitheater to his right and the five brothers in a row beside her. As Jon, Love o lay, Jack, and I come to the front, I stand next to Joseph on his left. The whole congregation stands and cheers. I don't know what is happening or exactly why, but it is a beautiful celebration and honoring. I now see flowers floating through the air with colorful butterflies flitting in and out, playing. I hear bright and perky music—I want to say pan flutes, but I think I am getting carried away with my imagination, pulling in everything I have ever heard about.

Joseph: This is all for you, Barbara. It is your homecoming party. All those you have ever met in the Amphitheater are here, even Mouse Woman and Sheela na Gig. We all celebrate. This is the true beginning. I wish now to speak to you in front of the whole congregation and holy gathering of beings who live and visit this land. We rejoice with one heart that you have at last come home to your Faerie family. Now we can truly step forward as a healing force for the planet. You are the final link in the collection of beings who know and relate with this land.

- The Librarians are here.
  (They all stand to be greeted by the congregation.)

- The Druids are here.
  (A long procession of white-garbed beings enters from the vortex grove where I had joined them once in ceremony.)

- The elementals from the Chalice Well Garden and Cress Meadow have arrived, even bringing their gardener with them, honoring him since he opened his heart and intuition and offered you the honor of climbing down into Chalice Well when the water had been turned off for cleaning and preparing for Summer Solstice. db.

- Findhorn sanctuary angels are here, with the angel of Findhorn. The angels, elementals, and ancient ones from Iona have arrived, and those sparse ones who live on Mull that you loved and blessed as you drove over those lands. The Errid angels are here, and one apologizes for trapping you and removing your boot in a boggy soft spot. These are the ones you related with in your spirit body when you stayed and slept on their lands. These are the Faerie folk.

- A message was sent from Ireland's holy hill, reminding you of its greetings as you walked through the circle of trees to ascend the hill of Tara.

- The Mother River Boyne also sends her greetings and reminds you of the stories she told you when you were quiet in bed, recovering from your broken leg—stories of your home on her shore, your service, and the healing of people, land, and waters that flowed out of the earth downstream under the name Boyne. db.

Although there may be others here whom I have not named, like the ones from Mays Howe on Orkney and the land you re-entered in the ancient site that had just been discovered, all know of your return to Faerie.

Please, dear BarBara, gently, quietly, take it all in. This home-coming has been going on for a long, long time and even beyond this life, when you lived in the forests of Europe, carrying the Mother's love to the animals, elementals, and humans. That, now, is what we all bask in as we stand here with you.

The love of the Great Mother
That flows through your breath
And blesses the land
Step by step
Breath by breath.

This you have been unaware of and I speak now so it will be enriched by your own conscious knowing of the blessing that you carry into the surface of the world. You truly carry the scepter of the Mother's divine love. That actually matches the scepter you saw me carrying when you saw me come out of and over the hill to greet you, carrying my own scepter of divine love when we met at Lolani's 12 years ago, in March 2004.

Barbara: I stand and greet you all, with great love and amazement. I delight in the memories of the lands I have traveled and loved, the land I lived on with you and loved, even though I was not totally conscious of what I was doing. I open my heart and hands and send love out to fill this space and each of you to the degree that you desire.

Joseph, I turn to you in gratitude for your gentle awakening and patient handling of my awakening process. I am here to be of service, to live in the consciousness of Faerie and open to learning and incorporating, reviewing and remembering what was set aside so long ago. And to you dear Jon, my partner and twin flame, I stand in union with you, for you know the way of Faerie and I look to you to guide our service to the planet and all that we are to do.

Oh, I am aware of Saint Germaine walking up the aisle in his violet robe and an aura of violet light. Dear Father, I welcome you to this wonderful celebration. Thank you for joining us.

Saint Germaine: I come to speak for the Seventh Golden Age and the empowering of all here to do the part each has signed up to do, to bring the changes necessary to save the planet and the people. Come home to this land when you need restoration and courage to go on with your work. db.

Come and rest and be nurtured in the Mother's love and my violet transforming flame. I, along with Amud ha Esh, establish here and now a nourishing, consuming violet flame in the center of this Faerie temple. Come and be nourished, one by one as you are led, then carry that violet flame home with you to give you sacred space and to create sacred space as you travel.

All is well. All is complete. All is done in good heart and good timing.

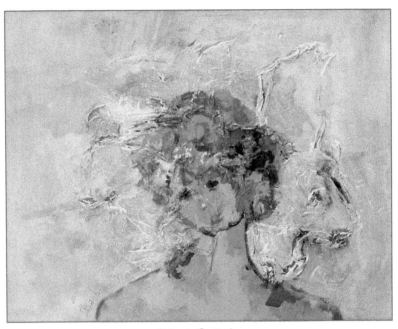

Living in Gratitude